Other clothing makers just don't measure up to Liz Claiborne, Inc.
Fortune Magazine

A legend of the apparel industry, taking a relatively unknown company and making it one of the largest in the United States
Women's Wear Daily

Chazen has a great feel for what the typical department store customer wants
Forbes

The architect of the Company's spectacular growth
New York Times

Industry people familiar with Mr. Chazen say his role over the company's marketing and merchandising and his close ties to retailers have been pivotal to the company's success
The Wall Street Journal

You have achieved a remarkable and wonderful career and truly created an international institution *Marvin S. Traub, President, Marvin Traub Associates*

Let's face it Jerry, you're a living legend in the field of retail. You are a well respected individual in the industry with a lot of history behind you. Without a doubt, you are going to be a tough act to follow
Allen Questrom, Senior Advisor, Lee Equity Partners, LLC

Under your stewardship, Liz Claiborne has achieved storybook results. While you have always given credit to others for the extraordinary success of the company, the industry knows that, without Jerry Chazen, Liz Claiborne could not have happened
David C. Farrell, Former Chairman & CEO, May Department Stores

My Life at Liz Claiborne

How We Broke the Rules and Built the Largest
Fashion Company in the World

A Business
Memoir by
Jerome A. Chazen,
Founder, Liz Claiborne, Inc.

authorHOUSE®

AuthorHouse™
1663 Liberty Drive
Bloomington, IN 47403
www.authorhouse.com
Phone: 1-800-839-8640

First published by AuthorHouse   12/8/2011

ISBN: 978-1-4670-3605-4 (sc)
ISBN: 978-1-4670-3604-7 (hc)
ISBN: 978-1-4670-3603-0 (e)

Library of Congress Control Number: 2011916304

Printed in the United States of America

To Simona,

My wife and partner, who has been at my side for more than 60 years. You have endured moves, bad times, life changes and more.

Thank you darling. It couldn't have happened without you.

Acknowledgements

I must admit that the impetus for writing this book began with my grandkids. They asked a lot of questions about the company and how it grew and then pushed me to write about it. So to Ross, Jeremy and AJ Banon and Zach and Anna Miller, thank you – your interest inspired me to take the plunge. My newest grandchildren, Jasper and Fiona Chazen, are only 4 and 2 years old respectively, but I hope they will enjoy this book when they are old enough to read.

As I began to collect material and gather memories of those days, I spoke with a host of friends and business buddies, all of whom contributed to the success of Liz Claiborne. The following are all retail CEO's who became our best customers and, in many instances, some of my best friends. I could probably sit and write a book about each one of these people and the stresses, strains and successes of our relationships.

Burt Tansky, who was probably the most responsible for building our business at Saks and then wouldn't put the line into Neiman Marcus because it wasn't expensive enough.

Mike Gould at Bloomingdale's, who I write about in the book, is the consummate retailer from his earliest days at Abraham & Strauss to his current position as CEO of Bloomies. He replaced the indefatigable Marvin Traub, who helped us in our earliest days and made us an important part of Bloomingdale's. Marvin left Bloomingdale's and started a new career as a consultant and is still running around the world.

Ron Ruskin, who has become a favorite lunch companion, was very important as a CEO in a number of companies and most especially at Batus/Saks.

Bill Dillard, who had such a thick Arkansas accent that when we first met I had to ask him to repeat everything at least once. Very proudly, I believe that the Liz Claiborne company almost singlehandedly moved Dillard's from a sleepy chain in Little Rock to a dominant department store force nationwide.

David Farrell, the CEO of the May Company and, in his day, perhaps the single most powerful and feared retailer in the country. He was a genius with the greatest store of information about every facet of every business in every one of the May Company stores. If he ever made a mistake, I never heard about it.

Bob Friedman, who I talk about in the book a little bit, during his Bamberger's days, stayed with the Macy's organization for many years and then ended up running Loehmann's. He and his buddy, Art Reiner, who was President of Macy's NY, were both smart and aggressive. They and their organizations kept pushing our company to heights we didn't know we could achieve.

Allen Questrom ran so many different retail organizations that it's kind of tough to remember, but I always think of Allen as a Federated person. We shared innumerable conversations, and I always consider him to be the kind of guy who gave all the credit to everyone in his organization and none to himself.

Terry Lundgren, who is currently the CEO of Macy's, Inc., the department store behemoth that virtually controls the industry, was an up and comer during the years of my book. We were always friendly and have remained so even more after I left Liz.

Tom Gould, from whom I get a call every Christmas, was the CEO of Younkers. Younkers was also the store where we, the Liz Claiborne company, generated, in certain years, almost 8% of their total business. It was almost as if this was a Liz department store.

Howard Socol, who was CEO of Burdines, was the key person in helping us develop a southern strategy so that while we were selling woolens up north in the winter, we would have appropriate fabrics for Florida and the rest of the South. Howard became a very close friend and, after leaving Burdines was a very successful CEO at Barney's.

Arnold Aronson – CEO of many major companies including Bullock's, Wanamaker's and Saks Fifth Avenue. He is now a consultant at Kurt Salmon Associates.

The Liz Claiborne corporate people all helped bring back facts that I used in the book. I would like to particularly thank the ladies responsible for sharing bits of their lives on these pages: Linda Larsen, Jan Sommers, Carol Hochman and Karen Greenberg. They not only were terrific employees, they have all remained good friends over the years.

I would also like to thank several key employees. Harvey Falk, who came into the company early on, really professionalized our financial end along with his most important deputy, Sam Miller. They were both very helpful in filling me in on some of the statistics and financial developments that had taken place during those heady years.

Jack Listanowsky was remarkable in remembering how many different countries we were in, how many different products we manufactured and were able to ship and how the entire process fell into place. I thank him for helping to flavor the book.

Of course, Ken Ganz, one of our earliest employees, remembered so much about the growth of the company. He reminded me of so many different stories that were all fascinating. I couldn't use them all, but I certainly enjoyed listening to them again.

I see Nina McLemore frequently. I have become a board member of her fashion company, and we talk about the old days constantly. All of the elements of our getting into the accessories business were particularly important for the growth of the company so, thanks again for all your help, Nina.

Hank Sinkel, salesman extraordinaire, is someone that I speak to quite often. He moved around to other companies, but my conversations with him were always about the good days at Liz.

Jane Randel was a youngster in our marketing area who was given the responsibility of helping to get the Liz Domestic Violence project off the ground. I see Jane now at the quarterly Liz Claiborne foundation meetings.

We do spend most of our time on the future, but since the foundation board consists of all Liz employees, at least some of whom were with the company before I left, there is always a certain amount of nostalgia. Jane is still doing a great job with the total marketing of the company and the domestic violence initiative.

Another member of the foundation board is Elaine Goodell, who helped a lot in digging up some of the old annual reports and proxy statements that I couldn't find.

As I was putting the book together, I reached out to Sherwin Kamin, Lou Lowenstein, Kay Koplovitz and Ann Fudge. Both Sherwin and Lou passed away while this book was being written, but the two ladies, our first women directors, are thriving and reminded me of many of the interesting board sessions. One of Lou's biggest contributions as a board member was his passionate belief in corporate governance. He made it one of the principles of his legal career, and I guess he wanted Liz Claiborne to be a poster child. We did set a very high standard. The one that affected me most was the early decision we made that no executive could stay past the age of 70. I thought it was a great idea and, unfortunately, before I knew it, I reached that age myself. Lou and I used to joke about it on the many occasions that we got together. It was the right thing for the company and, frankly, it was the right thing for me as well.

There are so many other people I would like to acknowledge, but I am afraid to mention some and not others. Every time I see folks, we start reminiscing, and it's as if we never left.

A few years ago, Leonard Boxer decided to put together a short biography, specifically for his family. Of all the founders, Leonard and his wife, Anita, are the two who became closest to Simona and me. We spent many wonderful times together, stayed with them in their home in Florida, attended all their children's functions (as they did ours) and were best friends. Leonard is gone now, but we still see Anita and the children. I used to joke that Leonard spent too much time reminiscing about the old days, but I could have used his help as I wrote my book. Anita, for her part, has been very helpful remembering some of the early days when she would come to help us keep the books in the company.

I write about Liz and Art in the book and the relationship I had with the two of them. Liz's passing was a very sad day for me, as were those last brutal years when she was diagnosed with cancer. Art Ortenberg and I drifted apart. He wrote a book, sort of an homage to Liz rather than a history of the company. In some ways, my book, besides being my side of the Liz Claiborne story, can be seen as an accurate portrayal of the growth and legacy of the company.

I also would like to thank the dozens, if not hundreds of people, many of whom I have met at various dinner parties and functions over the years, who remember Liz Claiborne as customers. When they find out about my background, they want to know how it all happened. I hope that when they read my book, I will have done a good job answering their questions.

Of course, I can't forget about Mona Mayer. Mona has been my assistant for over 20 years, and she is not only a historian of company events, but she has been indispensable in my writing this book and in the constant editing that has taken place. She has put together so many different versions and somehow kept everything in order.

Finally, I'd like to thank Dave Conti, who worked with me for well over a year, helping me to put this book together from day one. His writing, editing – and listening – skills are unparalleled. We had innumerable conversations during our time together, discussing my life, my career, and my memories of the company. Together we captured and committed to paper a story that I hope my readers find interesting, exciting and inspiring.

Contents

Introduction

In 1975 I was working at an apparel company called Eccobay, a manufacturer of low-priced separates for women. I had been there for about two years and wasn't very happy with the job, but I was making a very decent salary. I was also a partner in a small woman's clothing store in New Jersey called Casual Fair. The store had been a big hit, and between it and my day job, I was very busy and working, as they say these days, 24 / 7.

One day the phone rang. It was my old college roommate, Art Ortenberg.

Art, my wife, Simona, and I had all gone to the University of Wisconsin. Art and Simona had actually known each other since high school in Newark, New Jersey. I knew neither of them when I first arrived in Wisconsin. In fact, I didn't know a soul. But that quickly changed. I was walking down a street in Madison one day when I heard somebody yell out, "Hey, aren't you Jerry Chazen?" It turned out to be a fellow I knew from summer camp by the name of Gene Teich. I smiled. At least now I knew one person at the University! I told Gene that I was looking for a room to rent for the school year, and he mentioned that one of his friends needed a new roommate because the previous one had just been drafted (this was all taking place in the middle of World War II). The friend with the empty bed turned out to be Art Ortenberg. I took the bed that was available, and we became friends. Art later introduced me to Simona.

After college, Art and I stayed in touch and saw each other often over the years. Art had married his college sweetheart, fathered two children, divorced and then married Liz Claiborne. He and she seemed to be very happy together.

When I answered my office phone that afternoon, Art said, "Can you meet Liz and me for a drink?"

"Sure," I said, agreeing to get together with them that very evening. From the tone of his voice I knew something was up, but I had no idea what.

After work, we met at Bill's, a small, old fashioned restaurant and bar in the Garment Center on West 39th Street. The place was a favorite watering hole of people in the garment industry where we would meet colleagues for lunch or drinks after business hours. It looked like it was built 100 years previously and never renovated.

When we were settled in the booth with our drinks, I asked Art, "What's up?"

He replied, "Well, we've got a problem."

Actually, they had two problems. Art was running a small consulting company, and he had one account, a division of General Mills, that was giving him most of his income. General Mills had an incubator system for trying out new concepts and businesses that might be added to the company. Art had been chosen to develop one such business idea: clothing-making kits to be sold to women that included a pattern, the already-cut cloth, plus all the accessories such as buttons and zippers that she'd need to make the garment. He had worked on the business for a couple of years, but General Mills had determined that the volume potential was very limited and decided to abort the effort. That was the end of 95% of Art's income.

The second problem was Liz's company. She was a designer for Youth Guild, a dress company that had been purchased by Jonathan Logan, the giant clothing conglomerate. When the entrepreneur who had founded Youth Guild left, the company started to go downhill. And it continued downward to the point where Logan decided to close it. So Liz was going to be out of a job as well.

It turned out that the purpose of our meeting was to discuss their situation and see if we could come up with any good ideas for them so that they could continue to make a living.

As an ex-retailer and a more than casual observer of the fashion scene, I had spotted a trend that I felt could be meaningful and perhaps even revolutionary, and I decided to mention it: While dresses had dominated the apparel industry up until then, things were changing. There was a woman out there who was turning away from dresses and looking for the opportunity to put together different outfits by mixing and matching separates. (We would talk about this woman a lot later on.) I believed that the right kind of company jumping on this trend could be a big success.

In talking to Art and Liz about this, I was outwardly suggesting a solution to their employment situation, but subconsciously, I think I was putting myself in a position to be part of this company if it were really to happen.

I turned to Liz, who had spent almost her entire career designing dresses, and I said, "Do you think you can design for that woman?

Liz thought about it for a couple of seconds before she answered, "Yes, I know I can." She paused for another moment and continued, "Besides, I think I am that woman." It was only later that we discovered how important her identification with that woman would be to our future.

I knew Liz was an accomplished designer. I knew that the work she was doing at Youth Guild was excellent, and I respected her tremendously. Even though she had been designing dresses for many years, I believed she was quite capable of designing anything else she put her mind to, including separates.

Art was listening carefully and saying little. It seemed like he was trying to work out the possible ramifications of our conversation. We ordered another round of drinks and after they arrived, his first comment was, "So now what do we do?"

I blurted out, "We can start a company." I surprised myself with that answer – it just seemed to pop out of my head.

It was much more than a Mickey Rooney – Judy Garland movie. We were not kids when this conversation took place. We weren't three young people recklessly starting out on a naive adventure. I was 48 years old and a successful executive. They were about the same age: Art six months older and Liz one year younger. The three of us had spent virtually our entire lives in the fashion industry. We all had had our triumphs and made our mistakes. We were experienced industry veterans.

We relaxed, had a few more drinks, talked some more about this momentous opportunity, and came up with a plan. We would need money, and while the three of us could put some up, we knew we would need a lot of outside help. Art and Liz took charge of seeing if enough money could be raised among friends and family to get the business started.

That was the beginning of our great adventure.

The span of years that began with this conversation was the most exciting and fulfilling of my life. We started our company from scratch with a total investment of $250,000. We entered one of the most competitive industries in the country – one with a new company failure rate of 90%. Armed with solid experience garnered from employment in various apparel businesses, along with some good ideas about design and merchandising, my partners and I started our little company with a determination to do things differently. We were going to do things our way – with a willingness to break the rules of our very tradition-bound industry.

Not only did we beat the odds, we succeeded beyond our wildest dreams, growing in a very short time to become the largest fashion apparel company in history.

Beginning with our first few sales in 1976, we quickly accelerated to $23 million in 1978 and $79 million in 1980. After just eleven years in business, in 1987, we hit the billion dollar mark for the first time. By 1989 we were recognized as the largest women's apparel company in the country, with sales of $1.4 billion. In 1990, our sales were double those of our next largest competitor, Leslie Fay, and our profits were seven times theirs. We reached an astounding $2 billion for the first time in 1991, the same year we listed on the New York Stock Exchange. At this point we had almost 8,000 employees.

Over the years, we added dresses, denim apparel, accessories, fragrances, jewelry, menswear and much more to our original line of sportswear. Our manufacturing operation stretched across 50 countries around the world, and we produced 58 million garments and 18 million other products a year. We also began an international sales push in Canada and the United Kingdom, with plans to expand into Western Europe.

Liz Claiborne was named a Fortune 500 company in 1986, joining the list of the largest industrial companies in the US and one of the youngest to boot. In that same year, *Forbes* magazine declared us the # 1 most profitable public company in the US.

In 1990 we were ranked the #1 most admired company in the apparel industry by *Fortune* magazine. In 1991 we joined the top 10 list of America's most admired corporations at #10. We moved up to the #4 position the following year.

In today's world we hear stories about the explosive growth of one company or another in the high-tech sector, where a new technological marvel or internet idea can propel a company to gigantic proportions almost overnight.

But the apparel industry isn't like that. We weren't inventing a product the likes of which had never been seen and never been dreamed of. We were designing, manufacturing, and selling clothing as our predecessors had done for hundreds of years. Plus, while we were making our plans, developing our products, and marketing to our customers, so were hundreds if not thousands of other apparel manufacturers. And we all were competing to reach and attract the same consumer through the same group of department stores.

How in the world, then, did we do it? How did one company come to dominate an entire industry in such a short period of time?

In the past when I would reflect upon what we achieved at Liz Claiborne, I used to find myself wondering if our growth and success were not some sort of crazy accident of fortune. But with the perspective that the passing years have brought, I can see that it wasn't luck at all. It was hard work, a sharp desire to understand and supply the fashion needs of the American woman and a willingness to break the established rules of our industry. We operated differently, we kept our eye on the consumer, we challenged the practices of the past, and we changed the apparel industry forever.

I've written this book to leave behind a record of what we did and how we did it. I hope the Liz Claiborne story and my role in it will inspire others to dream big, work hard, challenge the status quo and always strive for excellence.

In the pages that follow, I've tried to give an honest and very personal account of the Liz Claiborne phenomenon, beginning with aspects of my early career that prepared me for my work at Liz, through the growth and expansion of the company, to my current status in "retirement" as an active philanthropist. My emphasis throughout, though, is on the ways we as a company continually innovated fashion, design, manufacturing, merchandizing, marketing – always finding new and better ways to do business, always with the goal of bringing the best possible clothing and merchandise to our consumer.

Chapter 1

The Opportunity of a Lifetime

In his book, *Outliers: the Story of Success*, Malcolm Gladwell describes the way very successful people can spend years and years working at something that helps prepare them for grabbing the right opportunity and creating spectacular successes – often what others might mistakenly see as "overnight success." Bill Gates, for example, spent thousands of hours working with and learning about computers and software from the time he was in middle school, experiences that helped prepare him eventually to found Microsoft; the Beatles performed hundreds of times in clubs in Liverpool and Hamburg, developing their musical talents and honing their performing skills, getting themselves ready to reach for the big time.

I'm not comparing myself to Gates or to John, Paul, George, and Ringo, but as I look back on my career and the incredibly swift success we achieved at Liz Claiborne, I know that it was no accident. It didn't just happen in some lucky, mysterious way. My partners and I had put in years of hard work in our jobs, always working for other people. We had gained three lifetimes – literally thousands of hours – of experience and knowledge, and now we were going to put all of that into our own company.

The comments I made to Liz and Art that night in 1975 were not frivolous or off the cuff. In many ways they were a reflection of the totality of my experience and background, including the fashion manufacturing knowledge I absorbed in a number of different jobs. But, perhaps most of all, they reflected the merchandising and marketing wisdom I had gained in retailing over the years.

I first started hearing about the apparel industry back in my college days at the University of Wisconsin from my good friend and fraternity brother, Alan Glen. Alan's family was from Milwaukee, and they owned what was then one of the largest apparel manufacturers in the country, Rhea Manufacturing. From the time I was in college with Alan, he thought it would be a great idea for me to come to work for Rhea. I would listen to what he had to say, but would always think, "I don't know anything about that industry. I'm really not interested in it." I had other plans. After I graduated from Wisconsin I went right on to Columbia University Business School, with the goal of landing a job on Wall Street.

Simona still had a year of college to go, but at the end of her junior year, we became engaged. After she graduated and I had completed my first year at Columbia, we married. Now she could get a job while I pursued an MBA.

I did well at Columbia where I was a finance and accounting major. My finance professor was a legendary teacher by the name of David Dodd. He co-authored, with Benjamin Graham, *Security Analysis*, one of the most famous and influential books ever written on investing. Professor Dodd helped me get my first and only job on Wall Street.

As I think back on my days at Columbia, a couple of significant moments come to mind. One was when I earned the only A in the marketing course that every student was required to take. I didn't think about it at the time, but I took to marketing like a duck to water – it just seemed natural and easy to me. The other had to do with the fact that, although I had majored in accounting and all of the Big Eight accounting firms in those days recruited on campus, not a single one would even interview me. I was informed confidentially that "no Jews need apply." The problem was with the accounting firms and not Columbia. The school had a high percentage of Jewish students in the MBA program and there was not the slightest bit of anti-Semitism evident.

I guess I should have realized that all this meant something, but I just didn't know it at the time. In any case, the courses that I took at Columbia and the knowledge of sound businesses practices that I gained and my affinity for marketing stayed with me and helped me enormously over the years.

After I received my MBA, I took a job on Wall Street. I became a junior analyst at a company called Sutro Brothers at 120 Broadway. The connection had come through Professor Dodd. Sutro was a Jewish-owned firm. My salary was forty dollars a week.

I enjoyed the job, although it seemed very elementary compared to some of the things we had learned at school. It was a very different Wall Street back then. We worked five and a half days because the market was open on Saturday morning. We had a tickertape machine in the office that was our only way of determining selling prices of the various stocks. There were four or five analysts in a relatively small room, for the most part, trying to answer questions that the firm's clients were asking.

At the beginning, the most difficult part of the job was memorizing all of the stock symbols, since the full company name was never printed on the tickertape. The brokers were all seated in a bullpen arrangement on another part of the floor. They all had their accounts, and the company's income was principally derived from commissions that clients paid for buying and selling securities.

As I got more familiar with the organization and the people, it became quite apparent that the path to success was paved with the business the stockbrokers brought in from their wealthy friends and relatives. I had plenty of friends and relatives but none of them were wealthy.

In the meantime, my college friend Alan Glen never stopped calling.

Eventually Alan and his uncle, Stanley Glen, who was president of the company, convinced me to go out to Milwaukee and see if I couldn't help them make Rhea grow in a really significant way. They had a dream that it could become a huge industrial corporation, comparable to other big businesses in the United States. At the time, Rhea's volume was only about $27 million, and even at that relatively small size they were thought to be one of the largest apparel companies in the country.

Simona and I had just gotten married, but since we had gone to school in Madison, Wisconsin, we had a lot of friends in the Midwest and felt we would be very at home there. So we packed our most important possessions, our stereo equipment and our records, and got into our 1949 green Plymouth and drove to Milwaukee, leaving our mothers to deal with the mundane problems, such as shipping our furniture. I left my career, my job on Wall

Street and any chance I might have had to become a big time financier. Every once in a while I do think what my life might have been like if I had remained at Sutro Brothers.

This was probably the first time I broke an established rule in business. Wall Street was the place you went to make your fortune, and getting a job there was next to impossible. And yet I walked away from it. New York was where everybody came to make their careers, to climb the ladder of success. So here I am instead leaving town and heading for the Midwest. I guess you could say that I was called away by the apparel business.

My job was supposed to be marketing. As I got to know the people at Rhea, they would say ""What are you doing here, what is it you're trying to do?"

I would answer, "Well I'm not really sure, but I think that I'm trying to do some different kinds of marketing."

These folks didn't even understand what the word marketing *meant*, but one of them said to me, "You want to understand this business? Become a salesman. Go out, get a line, show it to the retailers, learn what the problems are. Take what you get from dealing with them and convert it into understanding our business." That was probably the best advice I ever got.

The company carved out a territory for me in Illinois and Indiana (with the exception of Cook County, where Chicago is located and where you could really make money). My territory was filled with lots of small towns, lots of specialty stores and a few small department stores scattered here and there. The typical town had a population of about 25,000, and there were dozens of them in Illinois and Indiana. Each town would generally have two or three apparel stores that sold women's clothing.

I'd get up while it was still dark, leave the house at 5am on Monday morning and get into my territory probably four or five hours later, someplace in Northern Illinois or Northern Indiana. The trunk of the car would be loaded with samples of our current line. I'd be on the road and in the stores all day long, all week, and I would come back home usually on a Friday night. It would be 10 or 11PM by the time I got back. I did this for just about a year starting in the spring of 1952 and going to the spring of 1953.

One of the things that happened to me on the road is that I found myself asking the retailers in these shops a lot of questions, and I became genuinely interested in the way they did business and how their side of the fashion industry worked. I thought I was just storing up all this information so it would make me a better manufacturer down the road, but what really happened was that it made me more interested in the retailing side than in manufacturing.

I paid my dues on the road and did a reasonable job. The most important thing was that I was learning, soaking up experience and information and discovering my fascination with retailing – where the product meets the consumer.

When I came back off the road, the company thought that it would be good for me to get involved with the new, burgeoning children's division they had recently started. It was called Glen of Michigan; the Michigan name came in because the factory where the clothes were manufactured was in Manistee, Michigan, a town of 5,000 people. But everyone else, the designers, executives, and support staff was in Milwaukee.

Instead of making me just a salesmen, I was made sales manager. It was my job not only to sell but also to put together and manage a sales force. I did the job for close to a year. I was a kid, and I was hiring people much older than me. They would take the children's clothing samples and get in their cars and sell to the stores in the same way I had done. As a sales manager I was dealing with some of the larger accounts, so I got to know the department store people a lot more during that year. And l liked what I saw.

I used to travel to the Manistee factory almost every week. I had to take an overnight ferry from Milwaukee across Lake Michigan. It took about four hours to get across, sometimes dodging ice floes in the coldest weather, and I'd end up in a town called Ludington. There were sleeping accommodations on the boat, so I'd drive the car on and go to bed. The boat would start off at around midnight, and we'd get to Ludington about 4 AM but could stay on board until 6 AM. That way passengers like me could get a little sleep. From Ludington I would drive to the factory in Manistee. Our Glen of Michigan factory was the second largest employer in the town with 150 employees. The largest employer was the Morton Salt Company. We were on top of the salt mines in Manistee. I got to know the town pretty well. It was not an inviting place -- maybe okay if you were a hunter and you wanted to stalk wild game all day, but I was a New York kid, born and brought up in the Bronx, and I didn't care for it at all.

One day Lester Glen, the division head and another of Alan's uncles, sat me down and explained that it made no sense for the factory and warehouse to be in one city and the rest of the staff someplace else. The entire Milwaukee organization was going to be relocated to Manistee. "Jerry," he said, "it's time for you to move. I said, "Well, thank you for this wonderful opportunity, but no thanks. I've learned a lot here, and it's really been terrific, but it's time for us to part company," and I left Rhea.

Simona was pregnant at the time with our first child, Kathy, and I was out of a job. We sat down one windy day at a nearby beach and talked about the future. I shared with her – it was the first time I really expressed this to her or to myself – how strongly I felt about starting a career in retailing. I saw this as my opportunity to make the transition.

I told Simona that I thought we should move back to New York where I could look for a job at a department store. But she suggested instead that I speak to her boss. She had been working for a merchandise manager named Herb Leeds at the Milwaukee Boston Store.

I went to see Herb, and he listened to me and said, "No doubt you can get a job if you move back to New York. But before you go and do that, why don't you talk to our president? We have a very nice department store right here."

So I did, and the president hired me, putting me in a fast track training program. In a relatively short period of time I found myself an assistant buyer in the ladies dress department in the Boston Store's basement. Back then, every department store had a basement division where the lower priced goods were displayed and sold. Women willing to spend more on "better" clothing would shop upstairs.

I spent at least half of my time on the sales floor working with the salespeople and the customers and the other half making sure that the merchandise arriving from the various clothing manufacturers was being properly handled in our warehouse.

It was a time for learning, and I developed a deep appreciation of the needs of the department store consumer. Very often she came in with specific wants – a dress for a funeral, for example. (We never did have enough black dresses, as I remember to this day.)

I'd been doing this job this for several months when I got a call from the merchandise manager of the basement, a nice man named Spencer Kellogg. All the buyers reported to him. He asked me if I thought I was capable of taking on more responsibility. Here I was with my MBA and all my manufacturing experience, so I said, "Certainly," without knowing what he had in mind.

Mr. Kellogg continued, "Even though you've been with the store for a short time, I've watched you work, and I'm going to take a big chance with you. Effective immediately, you are promoted to buyer of the basement dress department." I was flabbergasted. I just couldn't imagine why I was moving up so quickly and what had happened to the current buyer.

It didn't take me very long to find out.

It turned out that the buyer was a rather strange person and had gotten herself into a lot of trouble. As I learned later on, she was stealing dresses from her own department. Store detectives had started following her. They eventually got a search warrant, went into her home where she lived by herself, and found literally hundreds of dresses hanging in every nook and cranny of her house. All had their original store tags on them. All were unworn, unused.

Needless to say, she was fired. And that's how I got my first job as a buyer.

The difference between being an assistant and a buyer was enormous – now I would be making all the buying decisions for the department. A buyer in a department store has pretty much the same responsibilities as the owner of an independent specialty store: all of the planning for sales and advertising, the hiring and firing of employees, placing orders for the merchandise, making sure it traveled from the warehouse to the floor in the most expeditious manner. At the time it felt like the culmination of all my dreams: Here I was, in a way running a business all on my own. I was responsible for every piece of it. It was like owning my own retail store.

The experience that I gained as a buyer has lasted me all of my life. I learned to appreciate the consumer and came to understand that, ultimately, she would be responsible for any success I enjoyed. I also learned a great deal about negotiating as I dealt with the myriad of manufacturers in New York and elsewhere. Sometimes we negotiated price; sometimes it was delivery;

and, sometimes, it was asking them to change a style so that, in my opinion, it would appeal more to my customers.

As young and as inexperienced as I was, to a very great extent I was on my own. I sat in those showrooms and made the decisions, and, eventually dealt with the consequences – good or bad. I was a small piece of a very large store, but I took my job seriously. It also gave me the opportunity when in New York to meet with other retail buyers from stores around the country, either in the offices of Federated Department Stores or in the various showrooms where manufacturers would introduce visiting buyers to each other.

There were probably dozens of buyers just like me, all with similar responsibilities, in dozens of department stores around the country. One of the only differences between us was the amount of volume we were doing – the dollar amount of sales in the department we were buying for. Volume depended a lot on what city you were in and how strong your store was. Your volume could be one million dollars or it could be ten million dollars. But beyond that, we were all pretty much doing the same job.

One of the first things I learned was that retail executive hiring was very much a game of musical chairs. Buyers moved around a lot because getting the next promotion, moving up, usually meant moving out – taking a new position in another store, probably in another city. It's still true today. If you examine the backgrounds of current department store presidents, family owned-operations excepted, each of them probably worked at four or five different retailers in different parts of the country before they made it to the top position.

In this almost cookie cutter environment, your volume became an important factor in how well you did financially. Management generally looked at buyers' salaries as a percentage of the volume in their department. The higher your volume, the higher your salary. One reason to move around and to look at positions in other stores had to do with increasing the size of your responsibilities – and your volume. It also had to do with positioning yourself to be able to climb the organizational ladder in your particular store.

As much as I loved my basement dress buyer job, I knew even then that I didn't want to be there for the rest of my life. I wanted to move to the level of merchandise manager, with buyers reporting to me, then to the next level, and if I was good enough, all the way to president of the store. That was the pecking order in retail, and my goal in life had now become making it to the top.

I was in my job with the Milwaukee Boston Store for about a year and a half when I got a call from a headhunter about a very interesting position at Lit Brothers, a big department store in Philadelphia. I went to Philadelphia, looked over the store, interviewed with management and was offered the job as basement dress buyer. This meant picking up the family and moving. While the new basement looked very much like the old one in Milwaukee, it was a big move up for me – another level of buying that would triple my current volume. Plus there were new challenges, as there was major competition to deal with from other stores in downtown Philadelphia. Since Lit Brothers was a much larger store, there were more chances for advancement.

In this new job, instead of a buying trip to New York once every month, I made two trips a week to the city to do my buying. It gave me a chance to be on top of what was happening in the world beyond my basement. It was a much more exciting way to work. I liked it a lot, got to know many other people in the business and learned a great deal.

I seemed to be a natural for retailing. I loved trying to understand the customer and buying the kind of clothes she would go for. I was constantly on the floor interacting with her and learning from her. I was able to develop a reputation with the key manufacturers as a thoughtful buyer whose criticisms and suggestions were worth listening to. I really enjoyed offering them ideas on types of merchandise they should make or ways to improve existing items and then seeing the item created, at least in part, on my suggestions. This whole process became what I enjoyed most about my job, and as we will see later in the book, it stood me in good stead throughout my career.

We didn't have computers back then. Instead, dresses were tagged with two-piece tickets. When we sold a dress, we would tear off half the ticket – the stub – and put it in a box. This became our record of everything that sold that day. I used to take those stubs home with me every night. I had a book with all my dress styles in it, and I would enter the sales for each style based on the stubs that had accumulated. The stubs only had numbers on them, but I would make it my business to know which style each and every number

9

stood for. If I couldn't remember what, say, style 2842 was, I would make a note and look for it the next morning when I got back to the store.

When I was done entering all the stubs, I would go through the book and see what was selling and what wasn't. I might think, "Gee, I didn't sell any of this dress and it's been on the floor a week. Something's wrong. They don't like it for some reason." This is what I did every day. And if I had to work until midnight or one in the morning doing my stubs, I did it. It never felt like work to me.

I was putting in long hours – days, nights, weekends. I loved it. I was working a full six days a week. The only reason I didn't work on Sundays was because the stores weren't open on Sundays back then.

Eventually I worked my way out of the basement and was promoted to buyer of junior dresses upstairs. Juniors was an important department in the store. I climbed those stairs out of the basement and into the light. I could see the sun, finally.

I was in that job for two and a half years when I got a call from a recruiter with an unusual opportunity: a company called Winkelman's, a chain of women's specialty stores headquartered in Detroit, needed a managing buyer for their entire dress division. While I would have some buying responsibility, I would also be supervising three other dress buyers. The company sold "better" women's clothing – the kind of goods you'd find upstairs in the quality department stores. At the time they had about 80 stores in the Midwest, but the buying office was in New York. I met the president, Stanley Winkelman, who was the son of the founder and whom I liked a lot. It was a good opportunity, and it meant we would be back in New York.

But here again, I was breaking a rule of the industry. As the general merchandise manager at Lit Brothers told me, "I know the company. It's a good company. But, I'll tell you something: once you leave the world of department stores, you're through. You can never come back."

I was shocked by his warning. "What do you mean?"

"They won't take you back. That's the way it is in the department store world. You've got to go from one level to the next, and you've got to be true to what you're doing within the business. Specialty stores like Winkelman's are a world of their own. So if this is the choice you're making, if leaving is what you want to do, I just want you to remember what I said."

Still, New York was very appealing.

I thought through all of the elements: Winkelman's was a bigger job, with an increase in salary. I'd have buyers reporting to me. And even though I wasn't a merchandise manager, my buying responsibility would be enormous. Plus, Winkelman's would be the largest customer for many of the dress manufacturers I'd be doing business with. That would give me a lot of clout, and I'd be dealing with executives at the highest level. In addition, because of its size, Winkelman's was able to create exclusive product for its stores, a job I relished participating in and something that was in fact my forte.

So Simona and I talked about it and she agreed. We had had our second child, Louise, in Philadelphia, and here we were pulling up stakes again. Of course we would be moving back to New York and family, but we had made many friends in Philly. We were nomads, but now nomads with two little girls, ages four and two.

It turned out that breaking this rule paid off in many ways, because my experience at Winkelman's became critical in terms of getting me ready for the eventuality of Liz Claiborne.

We did so many special, different things at Winkelman's that I had to work closely with manufacturing firms in ways buyers usually didn't. Instead of just going to showrooms and choosing among the items that the apparel makers had to offer, I was going out to them and even to the textile people themselves to get unusual projects done. The work provided me with a wealth of valuable experience. We were asking these people to make special cuttings for us and in many cases to buy special fabric for us.

Winkelman's had become famous in the market for semiannual special color promotions. We would choose a color that we thought was especially appropriate for a given season and that was different from the color ranges the manufacturers were showing. This required us to go directly to the textile mill and ask them to dye yardage for us that we would then divide up among the various manufacturers who were making our garments. It got me much more deeply into the world of textile design and manufacturing and helped to make me a well-rounded fashion person.

My day-to-day responsibilities were both to buy and to supervise the buying of dresses in accordance to requisitions I received each week and sometimes each day from the folks in Detroit who had the responsibility for planning and distributing everything we bought in New York. The merchandise manager in Detroit (my boss) also planned all the advertising and pretty much ran the whole operation.

I did the New York buying job for a couple of years. At that point a ladder-climbing opportunity arose in Detroit, where the merchandise manager position became available due to growth in the company. I was asked to fill the job. This promotion meant that our family would have to move yet again.

We were finally settled in New York, my hometown, after living in all these different cities around the country, and now it was time to pick up and leave again. I approached Simona with some trepidation mixed in with my excitement for the new job. "Honey, the good news is that I got promoted. The bad news is that the job is in Detroit. It's time to move again." Simona was great – she was fine with the move. So we left New York for Detroit. This was in 1960, and shortly after the move, our third child, David, was born.

The Winkelman organization was set up with a store group on one side in charge of design, personnel, and general sales management. The merchandising group took care of product planning, buying and advertising. It didn't take long for me to realize that my years of floor experience and actual consumer contact were a distinct advantage in the day to day running of the business and a competitive edge with the other executives in my division.

In my new role, I began another activity that would eventually be strategically essential for the work at Liz Claiborne: I started to travel overseas buying goods for the company. I usually went twice a year for three weeks each time. We were doing particularly well in developing a knitwear capability in Italy for the manufacturing of our dresses. We also bought in Austria, France, and England.

Production in Italy was interesting to say the least. We did hand knits there, made on small hand looms. The so-called manufacturer would buy yarn and pass it out to people in the village who had hand-knit machines in their homes. He would weigh the yarn and would give a worker, say, 20 lbs of yarn. The worker would go home and knit the garments, and she'd better bring back 20 lbs of sweaters, not 19 ½ lbs, because otherwise she would be penalized. That was the way the system operated in those days.

Along the way, we did a great deal of experimenting and testing. The factories would make samples to show us, putting together a pocket from this jacket, a collar from this one, trying to make them as American-looking as possible. Both sides had to learn and adjust. For example, one of things I learned dealing with the Italian knitwear manufacturers was that they had a different way of looking at sleeve length than we did. If I specified a long sleeve or short sleeve they would invariably make it too long or too short. So I started specifying ¾ sleeves because if they made it a little longer – ok, a little shorter – ok. Either way, we could manage.

Trips overseas would also include gathering ideas for our designs. I would go visit stores, buy samples, sometimes adapt what we'd find locally for the US market. We would also trade ideas with our manufacturers, coming up with designs or improvements to designs that worked for both of us. We would also from time to time send over our bestsellers to see what they could do with them.

Through this effort I learned about doing business overseas and how manufacturers there were very much like manufacturers in the States: some were good, some were bad, some could be trusted and some couldn't. I learned to distinguish the wheat from the chaff.

Twice a year, in company with Stanley Winkelman, I would visit some of the couture firms in Paris, where we would see their latest creations. We couldn't buy any of those very pricey garments, but I did learn a lot about the couturier world. This was during the period, in the 1960s when several US manufacturers began purchasing Parisian styles and offering their own versions to customers at very affordable prices. By and large it was a New York game, with Saks, Lord & Taylor, and Ohrbach's being major players. It created a lot of excitement as the most fashion-oriented people in New York would rush out to see the new garments based on the latest Paris fashions. Winkelman's became the Midwestern showcase for this activity. It was very exciting with everyone trying to be first to market with newest designs. But when the dust settled, nobody made money on this kind of activity. The phenomenon lasted for four or five years, but then it all stopped. The fun was over.

In 1960, I made my first trip to Asia where we were buying accessory products, gloves, some sweaters, but not yet apparel. I represented the company and the other merchandise managers who would tell me the kinds of things that they were looking for. I would travel, searching out the products, sometimes just getting samples, other times actually giving the manufacturers orders for the product that the merchants told me that they needed.

We were very, very early in terms of manufacturing garments in Asia. There were just a handful of American companies that were doing any business there at all. I got to know many of the manufacturers in that part of the world and came to understand how to find the best of the lot for our purposes.

I made two trips a year to Hong Kong and the Far East starting around 1960 and continuing through 1968. Hong Kong then was an emerging Third World country. I remember the sampans in the harbor, the lines of wash stretching from the windows of the apartment houses as far as the eye could see. Despite the poverty I saw, I was very impressed by the intelligence and work ethic of the Chinese manufacturers in Hong Kong.

We accomplished a great deal and were very successful in our stores with the merchandise that was made for us. Not only that, but the prices we paid for merchandise in Europe, and especially in the Far East, were much lower than what we would have paid for similar items in the US. We were able to bring much of this price difference down to the bottom line.

I would work with agents who specialized in bringing buyers and manufacturers together. They would take us around to the factories and showrooms and serve as interpreters. Our first agent in Japan was an American gentleman who had served in the US Army in Japan and loved the country so much he decided to stay there. He spoke Japanese fluently.

I'll never forget my first trip to Japan, where I was introduced to potential vendors. I was working in the sample room with a sweater manufacturer who was speaking Japanese to me which of course I didn't understand. The agent was sitting there listening to all this and explained that the salesman was telling me that he didn't want to seem pushy but was suggesting that if I liked the sweater I was looking at, could I please give him an order today. When I asked why the rush, he explained that he had an appointment the next day with the Russian sweater buyer. It turned out that there was only one buyer for all of Russia and when he placed his order it would be for many thousands and thousands of dozens, tying up the factory for months. The man wanted to work with me, but he wouldn't be able to unless I beat the Russians to the punch. I thought this was very funny and placed our small order, and it sold well back in the States. I never found out what the Russian buyer did. This was in the time of Communism and central planning in the Soviet Union. It's odd to think about it this way, but nowadays, with all of the mergers and consolidations of retailers, especially among the department stores, you can sometimes get the feeling that there is only one buyer in our country as well. If a buyer at one of the giant department store chains doesn't like the sweater you manufactured, you can forget it – you're done!

As a result of these experiences, I had a high level of comfort doing business overseas. Years later at Liz, the decision to manufacture our garments abroad became extremely important to the company. And my knowledge of overseas production is what drove the decision.

In 1968, Howard Olian, one of the textile manufacturers that I had worked with over the years, asked me to lunch during one of my New York trips. Howard was about my age and had a very successful firm with mills in New England, selling fabric primarily to women's apparel companies. He was interested in expanding Westwood, his business, and eventually going public. He told me that there was no one in the company, including himself, capable and knowledgeable about everything necessary to achieve these goals. He wanted me to join the firm, virtually as his partner, with the promise of substantial stock options.

I had been at Winkelman's almost eleven years and was now general merchandise manager of the company and executive vice president, with all the other merchandise managers reporting to me. But I felt I had gone as far as I could. Even though it had gone public, Winkelman's was still for all intents and purposes a family company, and Stanley Winkelman, who was only a few years older than me, was president. So in my mind I had climbed as far up the ladder as I could, and it was time to go.

Paradoxically, in my final discussions with the folks at Winkelman's, they did offer to make me president. But I realized that it would only be a grander title for the same job, and that Stanley would always be my boss.

When I told my Dad, a businessman himself, about my decision, I thought he would be pleased because the family would be moving back to New York. But, instead, he told me I was making a big mistake. My father had always been my role model. He had emigrated to this country as a young boy, had very little formal education, but was able to build a business wrapped around steam boilers. He installed them after removing the old boilers and profited largely by selling the scrap iron. It was a tough job, and he talked to me about getting an engineering degree so that I could eventually join him and help expand the business.

I never liked engineering, and I never really wanted to get involved in the kind of work he was doing. Instead, I took another route. Thankfully, though, my father was very supportive and happy with what I was doing in my career – although he never could figure out why I would want to leave Winkelman's. Actually, he thought I was crazy. I have reached the American dream. If I accepted Winkelman's offer, I would be president of a large company. But what he didn't understand was how much I was like him. He was running his own show. I needed to run mine, something I knew I'd never be able to do if I stayed.

The Westwood position had truly caught my imagination. What attracted me was the combination of getting back to New York City plus the challenge of expanding a small company and taking it public, giving me a chance at ownership.

Howard and I talked a lot. We went over the Westwood customer list – they were all firms that I knew and had done business with as a retailer. I could really enjoy working with them again, and I looked forward to being Howard's partner in this adventure.

I discussed the move with Simona, and she understood my motivation. She told me she knew I always needed new horizons to conquer. I had to do more than I was doing at Winkelmans. It was very difficult leaving Detroit, where we had many dear friends. It was also tougher on the family, especially our daughter Kathy, who was in her junior year of high school and didn't want to leave her friends in Southfield, the area outside of Detroit where we were living.

The nomadic Chazen family was at it again. As the loaded moving van pulled away, we got into our car with the three kids and two kittens, and Kathy wept.

Soon we were back in New York, and I began yet another new career, this time in the textile business. Kathy, incidentally, adapted beautifully, becoming active in the yearbook and snagging one of the most popular guys in her new high school as her boyfriend.

I, however, didn't do so well. I knew almost immediately that I had made a mistake. I kept thinking of my father's advice, but it was too late. Westwood was nothing like I expected. The business was very poorly managed, especially in comparison to Winkelman's, where we had a large, well-structured, well-run organization. Howard had essentially built an organization that catered to his personality, and it didn't look like he was going to change anything just because I was now with the company. He had never had a partner, only employees, and he was not used to sharing information and decision-making.

Howard became a different person once I started to work at Westwood. It was like I had never met him before – the warm, friendly relationship we had all but disappeared.

There was an incident that may have hurt the relationship right from the start. When we discussed my joining the company, and the fact that I would be buying a house, he urged me to look in Sands Point, Long Island, where he lived. He had a vision that we might be neighbors, would commute together, and could spend the time on the train talking about business and everything else, as we rode to and from New York City each day.

When Simona and I decided that Long Island was not where we wanted to be, I think Howard had his vision crushed, and it affected the way we worked together from that point on.

Westwood had purchased a small knitting mill in Charlotte, North Carolina, and Howard had hired two executives to run this part of the business. On my second day on the job, he called me into his office and told me there was a problem. The men he had hired were doing a terrible job. He said, "The sales guy couldn't sell his way out of a paper bag, and the production guy knows nothing from nothing. I want you to take over the knitwear division. I know you can do the job."

I thought, "My God!"

Suddenly I found myself in the unlikely position of managing a knitting mill in North Carolina, a job I knew nothing about.

I developed a routine: I would take a Monday evening flight that left New York about 5:00 PM for Charlotte. I'd spend all day Tuesday at the plant and fly back to New York on Tuesday night. I did that every single week.

I was responsible for the division's product as well as the sales. One saving grace was the manager of the mill, Ralph Kier. He was a wonderful gentleman who had started the plant after coming to the US from Cuba when Castro took over the country.

I learned an awful lot about running a company – almost a startup really – and making knitted fabric, including buying yarn, dying yarn, and everything else I could ever want to know about knitting. While I struggled with the knitting mill, I did enjoy building the business, but I knew I was in the wrong place. I had a five year contract, a decent salary, a lot of family responsibilities, but I knew that I would eventually have to make a move.

One of the clothing manufacturers that we were doing business with – selling fabric to – was Herb Chesler. He owned a company called Eccobay where he made moderate priced apparel that sold to department stores. Herb and I had a good relationship when we were doing business together. He liked the fact that I always approached selling my textiles from a retailer perspective. I always thought like a retailer and would ask, "What are you going to do with the fabric? What sort of garments are you going to make? Do you think this is where the consumers are right now?" I always had the ultimate consumer in the back of my mind no matter what part of the game I was in.

As my relationship with Herb grew, he kept telling me that I was in the wrong place, that I belonged in manufacturing, running sales and merchandising for his company. Herb's forte was production, and he felt that with my background, we would have a great partnership. I used the word "partnership" advisedly, because I always felt that being made an owner / partner in the business was an implied promise on Herb's part.

The minute my contract with Westwood expired, I left and joined Eccobay. This was in 1973.

When I made this change, I couldn't help thinking back to my very first job in the fashion industry at the Rhea Manufacturing Company more than 20 years earlier. I had been so many places and done so many things in between, but here I was, back in manufacturing. It seemed like all the other jobs and all the other experiences had been preparation for moving back into this side of the business.

I loved being in this part of the industry, working with retailers, dealing with the department stores, seeing the buyers every day in our showroom. I would always ask, "What's happening? What's going on in your stores? What's selling? What's not?" Because Eccobay was important to these stores, I would have access to the merchandise managers, not just the buyers. They had a better grasp of the big picture, of what was happening throughout the store. It was through them at this time that I started to realize that dresses, as a category, were beginning to look a little tired, and that separates seemed to be gaining a foothold. Of course, Eccobay was a separates company, and we were doing very well.

Up until this point in time, dresses were 90% of the women's apparel market. There really wasn't much in the way of sportswear. It was dresses, then coats, then suits. Sportswear was a very minor category, usually limited to vacation-oriented areas in the store. Dresses had been the uniform of the day for years.

But to borrow from Dylan, the times they were a-changin'. People were starting to live their lives somewhat differently. We were seeing a relatively more casual feeling in the way women were dressing, with nice dresses being reserved for special occasions.

As I usually did, I shopped the department stores to see what was happening. I was always in the stores. I couldn't stop. I didn't play golf. I didn't have other hobbies. It was almost a joke in the family. Simona used to ask me, "Don't you ever get enough of these stores?" But I couldn't stop. I don't know what was driving me, but I enjoyed it.

But I wasn't enjoying the rest of it. Herb had made promises about my becoming a partner in the business, but that never happened. But, still, I had an excellent salary and was happy with most other parts of my work, so I kept at it.

During my time at Eccobay, I received a call from my cousins, Edith and Norman Kutner, who owned a large cosmetic and drug store in Rockaway, New Jersey. The store was very successful, and they called to tell me about some vacant space in the small shopping center they were located in – a perfect spot, they thought, for a clothing store. I drove out to Rockaway, checked it out, and sure enough the location looked like a good one. I approached Herb about going into partnership with me in the store, and he agreed. I filled it with Eccobay product and clothing from some other manufacturers as well – all in the sportswear category. I had people working in the store for me, but I drove out there at least once during the week and every Saturday. And I was still carrying my full workload at Eccobay.

The store was a big success and it contributed additional income which, with two daughters in college and Simona back in school studying for her master's degree, became very helpful.

So in some respects things were fine – having a hand in retail again with the new store, plus the money was good. In other ways they were not so good –I couldn't help feeling that I was running in place and not getting any closer to where I wanted to be.

I think my frustration had to do with my wanting to be in control – to run a business my way. Of course, the only way to be completely in control of something is to own it, and I had spent my entire career working for other people. I had done a good job for everybody, and I had been well paid. While I certainly made many decisions in my areas of responsibility, still, I always had to consider how the CEO wanted things to be run. Unfortunately, in the companies I worked for most recently, I believed the CEO was wrong a lot of the time.

I began to think that if only I had stayed in retail I could have been a department store president by now, and that would probably have made me very happy. But it wasn't going to happen now, and I really didn't see how to change my life. So I just kept running.

Then I got that call from Art Ortenberg...

The business that Liz, Art, and I discussed that evening was the opportunity I had been waiting for – the job I had been training for all my life. Having a shot at running this company and making it a success was exactly what I wanted. The idea was so important to me that I couldn't even think about the possibility of failure.

It was my conviction that this could become the business of my dreams.

If I didn't take grab this and try to make it work, I would go to the grave feeling sorry for myself. This was *my* opportunity of a lifetime.

Chapter 2

Approaching an Old Business in a New Way

I wanted this new business. I knew we could make it happen.

We had an idea, some grand ambitions, and some good people: Liz was a talented designer; Art a knowledgeable textile man; I was a businessman-merchant-salesman. We needed a production man and put an ad in the paper that basically said, "Production manager with money to invest wanted for new company." Luckily for all of us, Leonard Boxer answered that ad. Liz loved him right away. She liked the way he was dressed; she liked the way he talked; she liked his ideas for the product. Plus, he had $25,000 to invest in the company.

We had a dream, but the reality was that we needed investors and money. Liz and Art came up with $25,000 each. Liz had an aunt she was close to who put some money in. Some manufacturers who knew Liz and respected her talent also invested. All in all we were able to scrape together $250,000 to start the business.

I was able to put up $15,000 initially, as I had two kids in college at the time, and Simona was in graduate school studying for a degree in social work. I had a mortgage and other big expenses and couldn't afford to do more. I couldn't afford to leave Eccobay either. I was jealous that I had to stay in that job for the time being, that I couldn't devote every waking hour to our start-up. So I moonlighted, working on the business every night until the wee hours and most weekends.

As soon as I was able to straighten out my finances, I left Eccobay and joined Liz Claiborne, Inc., full time in April, 1977. At last my dream of being in my own business was coming true!

Since I was coming in as an equal partner to Leonard, Liz, and Art, I felt it only right that I increase my investment in the company. They had each put up $25,000, and I'd only put up $15,000. It seemed fair that my risk be the same as theirs. They told me that I really didn't have to do it. But I did it anyway, putting in another $10,000. We became equal partners with equal shares in the company, and I was much happier about that going forward.

During the course of our first months, we held a number of meetings to determine what kind of company we would create and market and how it should be organized.

We had a lot of good things going for us, including a talented designer and a group of experienced, well-rounded fashion industry executives.

We also had an idea:

I had been describing to Liz and Art a new trend I was seeing. Women were beginning to wear separates, such as a skirt, blouse and coordinating jacket, rather than dresses. This was a big change. I believed that there was a consumer out there who was a very busy woman – she went to meetings, lunches, was active in her community and the PTA, and she needed clothes that worked well for such occasions. Separates gave her the ability to put together different outfits without spending a fortune on new clothes for every occasion. (This trend, by the way, predated the movement of women in the workforce that eventually became so important to our company. This was not yet a factor in 1975-76.)

We had our eye on this new consumer, and I believed that we could be in the business of taking care of her clothing needs.

On the other hand, we had very modest funds to work with in an industry loaded with firms looking to clothe the women of America. We would be one more of literally thousands of companies, nationwide, hoping to succeed in an industry with a 90% failure rate.

What would make us different? What would make us better?

These were the questions that we had to answer in convincing ourselves that we would be successful.

The case for Liz Claiborne went like this:

We would try to emulate the designer companies such as Calvin Klein, Bill Blass, Anne Klein, but offer our clothes at much more affordable prices.

We would put together a collection of coordinated separates, blouses, pants, jackets, and the rest, meant to be worn together. We would not take the traditional "single classification" approach that our competitors were presenting, meaning we would not specialize in just one type of clothing as most manufacturers did.

We would have a real person, a real designer's name on the label. "Liz Claiborne" had a great sound and a very American feel to it. It was so good that some people thought it was made up. But, as a matter of fact, Liz's family in the US dated back to before the Louisiana Purchase, and her great, great grandfather had been the governor of Louisiana. Not only that, but the main thoroughfare in New Orleans is Claiborne Avenue. Putting her name on the label of an affordable collection, as opposed to a high-price designer collection, was a new approach that already differentiated us from the pack.

We knew that typical designer garments were overpriced for our target consumer, because their low volume made high markups necessary. We would do it differently, with a relatively modest markup that would make our retail prices reasonable. We would make our profit on increased volume.

We would make quality clothing for women. We wanted our customers to be able to examine the jacket or the blouse and see and feel the quality and understand the value they were getting when they bought our products.

We knew how important fabric was as an indication of quality, and we would use designer equivalent fabrics as much as possible. Even the trimmings would be carefully selected so that buttons, buckles and such would have a luxury look.

The credo of the company from the very beginning would be "It's all about the product. Give the consumer the product that she wants, and she will respond."

I think that, strange as it sounds, the emphasis that we put on satisfying the consumer was a little unusual back then. Most apparel companies felt that they had to please the buyers who came into the showroom because those were the people who wrote the orders. I never believed that. Obviously, you have to get the order, but, even more obviously, if the consumer loves and buys your merchandise, the stores have to write the orders.

Leonard Boxer, Liz Claiborne, Art Ortenberg and Chazen in 1984.

A day at the office.

We decided that we would focus our efforts on the big stores. We'd sell to the department stores, mainly because that's where my background and experience was, and I believed that would make a big difference as we got started.

There was no hesitation on the part of either Liz or Art to agree to these ideas; now we just had to make it all happen.

We had a mission, and we also needed an organization. We needed to pick corporate officers. With two alpha males in the office – Art and myself – we both decided that in the best interests of the company we would step aside and Liz would become president. It turned out to be good PR. Feminism was in the air and having a woman as president gave us a particular cache. We agreed that Liz would have the title, even though we all knew that she wouldn't be performing the duties that the office required. Art and I agreed to take similar titles, starting out as executive vice presidents. At one point, we both became co-chairmen.

In spite of our friendship, and many good times together, there had always been a certain wariness in my relationship with Art. Even now it is difficult to explain. He was smart in college, articulate in discussing any number of intellectual concept, and seemed absolutely prepared to be a college professor – probably a professor of English. He was clever and had a witty tongue, but I never saw in him a particular appetite for business. Nor did he seem even to like the world of business. He was not a "natural" at it, while, for me, it came easily. His career had had its ups and downs, and he moved from position to position without leaving much of a mark. Perhaps this was the basis of his not always hidden resentment of me which would become more marked in years to come.

Art always had difficulty giving me credit for the key role I played in the company. I had to live with that reality then and for many years after, no matter how my ideas and my management guided the company to success. I guess that I was having so much fun it really didn't matter. But, to be honest, sometimes it did get to me. With Liz in the limelight, as we wanted her to be for the sake of the label, Art was always able to make sure that stories that came out about the business either downplayed my role or didn't mention me at all. I was sad to see that I was not even mentioned in Liz's obituary as her friend and one of the founders of the company.

We started out in a very small space at 80 West 40th Street, right across the street from Bryant Park and the New York Public Library. It was called the Bryant Park Studios and had been built around 1900 as combined working studio space and living space for artists. Because the Park was across the street rather than another building, it had beautiful open light. Our showroom was kind of artsy looking with extremely high ceilings and very large windows. It was a very old building with very old elevators that creaked on the way up and on the way down. In a way, the look and feel of the building added a little bit of mystique to this new company that was trying to do things in a different way.

We divided this miniscule space – it couldn't have been much more than 1,000 or 1,500 square feet – for our little operation. We set up one room for Liz to use as a design and sample making room. Art used another small room where he worked on fabrics. Then there was an oversized closet that we opened up and that became my office. There was no window, no anything, just enough room for a small desk and a telephone. There was a door, but I couldn't close it because there would be no air circulation and the room would become suffocating. In the balance of the space we put in a few small tables and chairs so that the buyers would have someplace to sit down. We had almost no staff. We did hire a bookkeeper. Where she sat I can't even remember. Leonard's wife, Anita, even came in from time to time to help with some of the bookkeeping chores, so it was a real family business. We set up a small warehouse in a converted garage in New Jersey, where we could receive and ship our goods.

At one of our first line planning meetings, Liz presented us with a large number of planned styles based upon the tradition of allowing the buyer to choose the ones she liked best. In most apparel companies, a designer typically designed a lot of pieces, and then samples would be made up from the designs to show the buyers. The department store buyer would come in and select which items she liked. Other buyers would do the same. Then the manufacturer would tally all of the orders, buy the necessary fabrics and then put the pieces into work – into production. The samples that hadn't been ordered in enough quantity to justify production were discarded. The process worked for two basic reasons: the fabrics and the clothing were all made in the US and so could be manufactured relatively quickly in time for whatever season they were showing. Second, no one was thinking in terms of presenting a coordinated line of separates to the consumer, so ordering a little of this and a little of that and skipping this one or that one wouldn't make any difference.

As we considered Liz's designs, I put myself back into "retail" mode and quickly realized that with our small capital and our mission to present a coordinated line, we were going to have to approach our design and merchandizing efforts very differently from the other apparel companies. We were going to have to break some rules.

We spent a lot of time discussing a new way of doing business: We would create a line of tight groups – pre-merchandised and virtually pre-selected for the buyers. "This is our line." If they liked it, they would buy the whole line. There would be no cherry-picking the collection. In this way, we would get past the buyer to our real customer – the woman shopper in the department store. She would be able to see and hopefully appreciate the "story" that Liz was putting together for the line, and she would buy our merchandise.

Liz got this concept right away and agreed to take this approach in her designing.

I remember vividly the day all this took place for a couple of reasons. It was the day we made important decisions that set a future course of the company. But it was also a sad day: while I was working with Liz and Art at the office, I received a call and was told that my father had had a heart attack and before he could even be taken to a hospital, he passed away. My father was 78 years old and, I thought, in perfect health.

So I'll never forget that day – Saturday, February 14, 1976, Valentine's Day.

I felt pretty strongly that the ideas Liz and Art and I discussed on that day would work – that the buyers would be able to handle us differently from the other manufacturers they were doing business with. Knowing buyers, having been one, having managed them, I thought they would jump at this sort of opportunity. One big reason was that it would make their job easier. If the merchandise looked good, they wouldn't care that we weren't letting them choose from a lot of different samples.

If this new way of presenting a line was going to be accepted, though, it meant that whatever we were showing had to be very, very compelling. We had to make the buyers come away thinking, " I'd love to have this in the store just the way you're showing it to me."

This was all revolutionary, but I was pretty certain it would work, even though the department store buyers had not bought this way before, weren't organized to do it and didn't present their merchandise to the customer this way.

In those days, stores had a blouse department, a pant department, a jacket department, a sweater department, and so on. A different buyer would be in charge of each department, and each of them knew their products and their manufacturers.

My first office- "closet" at 80 West 40th Street.

And at the time, 99% of these manufacturers were specialists, making goods only for one department. There were sweater makers, skirt makers, blouse makers and so on, all dealing with the buyer in charge of their particular product.

This became a challenge for us as we were taking on the responsibility of making all of these different products ourselves. Our blouses had to be as good and as competitive as the best blouse maker's blouse; our skirts as good as the best skirt maker's. So we had to be very, very good.

So our modus operandi became making small coordinated groups – each group to be purchased by the retailers in its entirety. A group generally consisted of a jacket, sometimes two jackets, a couple of skirts, three or four blouses and perhaps two pair of pants. The line was made in good colors, as color was Liz's signature. She had a terrific color sense and knew how to work with it. We didn't get into knitwear until about a year later. As the company grew, we added additional groups to the collection, but we never deviated from our tight offerings.

All our pieces were coordinated. So the advantage for our customers was that if she bought a skirt and a jacket, she could buy two blouses and then would be able to make two different looking outfits out of them. Or if she bought two skirts with the one jacket, she could mix and match and have a number of different outfits.

Our new way of presenting and selling to the retailers also required a new kind of sales force. We needed a salesperson who was willing to reject the traditional approach to selling, who wouldn't just show the buyer our line and then let the buyer say "Well, these are the items I like the best. I'll buy this and this, but I'll skip this and this." I just didn't want any more of this cherry picking, not if we were going to be successful.

We needed salespeople with retail backgrounds to move over to our side of the business, join with us and become our connection to the retailer. Occasionally people would move into our sales area without a retail background. We decided that educating them about retailing was so important that we established programs in conjunction with the Fashion Institute of Technology to teach them the principles that the retailers lived by, with particular emphasis on the math, so that they would understand the accounting, open to buy, markdowns, gross margin and other important concepts.

Linda Larsen: Early Days at Liz

In mid December of 1978 I walked into the offices of Liz Claiborne Inc., located at 80 West 40th Street, to interview for a sales position. It was a loft-like space, with huge windows the height of two floors overlooking Bryant Park. As "old world" as the building was, the Liz environment was modern with lots of white, very open, and divided by small white walls that defined the "work spaces." I could hear people laughing and singing..... something about "FRENCH TERRY"...! Later while interviewing with the Sales Manager, I learned that the staff was practicing their skit for the upcoming Annual Holiday Party to which the entire company was invited.

Tremendous energy and enthusiasm permeated the space and convinced me that this was the place to be. I was hooked! I knew from that moment that I wanted to be a part of what was going on at Liz Claiborne Inc.

I was hired by Jerry Chazen, one of the four founding partners of the business, and officially started my job at Liz the week after my interview.

But missed the big party! However, in the following weeks of preparation for Market Week, I became very familiar with French terry, velour, and many of the other fabrics that were staples of the Liz Claiborne Collection.

The company was much like a family in the beginning. Looking out over Bryant Park from our clean and modern offices, working with enormously talented people, and representing a company that it seemed like everyone loved and wanted to be a part of ... we were on top of the world. I remember those days as if they lasted much longer. It was a special place at a special time.

However, change was already in the air and during my first interview some of the plans were revealed to me. There was a huge architectural drawing of the new showroom and offices, under construction at 1441 Broadway, hanging in Mr. Chazen's office. The company had already outgrown the 40th Street location, and in the Spring of 1979, Liz Claiborne Inc. moved to new offices which spanned two full floors. Liz and her design staff on the 12th floor, and Sales, Merchandising and Production Staff on the 7th.

Hiring retailing people for our business was a big rule breaker. No apparel manufacturer that I was familiar with had ever hired a retailer to work in the sales area. The objection had always been that having them sell to the buyers would only lead to big problems. There would be too much empathy for the buyers' problems and the best interests of their new employers, apparel manufacturers, would not be represented.

This was a ridiculous assumption. I always assumed that our true customer was not the retailer, not the buyer sitting in front of us in the showroom, but the consumer who would be shopping in the store and selecting and paying for and wearing our merchandise. I guess that point of view was rare, as most manufacturers saw the retailer as their customer – that's who they wanted to please. I wanted a mindset that was concerned about the consumer getting the best possible selection of merchandise to make her happy. It was our mantra from the very beginning that, if the consumer likes our product and buys our product, the retailers will have to come back to us and buy. And fortunately for us that's precisely what happened.

Our next item of business was to figure out where the stores were going to display our line. Most didn't have a department for it, and we weren't going to let them scatter our clothes into the various classification departments. That would defeat the whole purpose of what we were trying to do.

Only Saks and Bloomingdale's had places where they could display our whole collection; no other stores in the industry did. They didn't have departments to show the merchandise. They didn't have buyers who could buy it. They just weren't set up to deal with it. The reaction of Ed Roberts, the president of J.L. Hudson Company, was pretty typical. He came in, looked around and loved what he saw. Then he said, "But what am I going to do with it?" This is the president of the store, so you'd think that if anyone would know, he would.

But I had spent all those years in Detroit and also knew a lot about the J.L. Hudson Company. I'd been in their Detroit flagship store dozens of times. I was familiar with the high-end designer shop in that store, so I said, "Ed, bring in the buyer from the Woodward Shop (that was the name of their designer department) and let her buy our line for the company. You'll find a place on the sales floor to put our collection. You've got big stores, and I know you'll be able to find just a little space for us."

He was a bit skeptical but, to his credit, he wanted to try it out. He said, "I don't know, but ok. We'll see what we can do." They did well, and the J.L. Hudson Company became one of our most important customers.

We had a similar experience with Bamberger's, which was a huge department store chain located mainly in New Jersey and the Mid-Atlantic States. It was part of the Macy's company. Bob Friedman, the president of Bamberger's, who I knew from my days at Eccobay, came in with his buyer and looked at our merchandise. I explained exactly what we were trying to accomplish, and he turned around with a quizzical look on his face, and asked, "So what would you like us to do?"

I immediately thought of Paramus. It was their highest volume, best performing branch store at the time, surrounded by thousands of upscale, suburbanite families. In my mind, it was just the demographic we were looking for.

"Just take a little area in the Paramus store, and it will be for the Liz Claiborne merchandise. We'll ship the collection, and we'll put it together in the store, set up some t-stands or racks, and let's see what happens."

Bob looked at me again and, "Okay, we'll try it.

This was a big moment for us. We put our merchandise into the Paramus store, and the reaction was phenomenal. The consumers loved what they saw and responded in the best possible way: They tried the merchandise on and bought it. It didn't take management very long to understand that something very special had happened in this little section of the store. Set literally in the middle of thousands of other garments, Liz had attracted consumers and gotten them to buy. There were no "sale" signs, no advertisements, just well-made coordinated garments.

The Macy/Bamberger group responded very quickly and wanted to replicate the Paramus test in other stores. Of course, it was very difficult for us because we hadn't really made enough product to handle all of the proposed orders, but the news of our success spread like wildfire.

What happened with Bob Friedman and Bamberger's can't be underestimated as a factor in the success of Liz Claiborne, Inc. I recently ran into Bob in a restaurant – we're both retired now, of course. I introduced Bob to a friend I was dining with, and said, "You know Bob might be responsible more than anybody else for the success of Liz Claiborne."

Bob was surprised. "What are you talking about?"

I reminded him of his first visit to the showroom, all the things that we had talked about, and the fact that he was willing to give us space in Paramus for our line. I said "You were a believer."

His response was gratifying and embarrassing. "Sure, Jerry But there's something that you must understand. I didn't believe in the merchandise. I believed in you."

I'll never forget that conversation. It meant a lot to me.

In any event, even with this initial success, our volume was relatively small. In 1976 we barely hit $2 million and grew by 1977 to $7.4 million. We were still in a testing mode for the stores. The buyers were open to our ideas and accepted the reasons we were showing the complete collection and asking them to buy it all. Most of these buyers were women, and in many ways they were also the person we were going after as a consumer. I think many of them pictured themselves buying this merchandise for themselves, and it made it a little bit easier for them to understand what we were trying to do. So even though it was unheard of to show a line consisting of fifteen or twenty different styles and then asking them to buy it all, it started to make some sense. Of course, once we got some good retail performance from the merchandise, it made the job much easier.

At this critical stage each of the partners knew and understood this new way of doing things. Everything had to be synchronized. Liz had to design into a total collection and make sure each garment had a relationship with other garments. This was very different from what she did in her previous work, where she was creating individual dresses. And of course she did it beautifully. Her design and color sense, combined with her ability to understand and respond to the needs of the customer made all the difference in the world. Art, as our fabric maven, had to make sure that the fabrics were compatible and that they were delivered to us on time and were color matched. And Leonard had to schedule the factories so that the entire collection could be made and shipped together. We couldn't afford to have an individual jacket or an individual skirt be two or three weeks late because that would upset everything we were trying to do. The consumer would not see the entire group the way Liz visualized it and the way we were trying to present it and sell it.

So the pressure was on, in a sense, from the very beginning to make sure that the company operated and functioned in a way to make everything mesh. Was it always perfect? Absolutely not. Was everything always exactly on time? Absolutely not. But we did the best we could, and we did a good enough job of delivering the collection intact and on time so that the consumer was able to see it the way we intended and to consider our offerings. As it turned out, consumers were thrilled with what they saw, and the stores were blown away by the results.

Our Logo

Buyers and consumers certainly bought into the Liz Claiborne name on the label, and it had become the most important point of identification for our clothes. But we felt that the company should also have some sort of identification on the outside as well – a tasteful signal that the consumer was wearing a Liz Claiborne garment.

Logos were popular in Europe, where the couture houses had developed distinctive marks and used them with great success. Chanel had the double C that everyone recognized; Hermes had a stylized H; Lacoste had its little green crocodile. Many other companies as well had identifying icons that they placed on their wares. In our country one of the most successful was Ralph Lauren's polo player, which he used on much of his merchandise, especially the sportier items. It had worked very well for them.

With a logo on the outside of a shirt or a handbag, the customer is able to show that she owns a certain brand of merchandise – something of quality that she could be justifiably proud of. And everyone who saw her would know it as well.

I loved the idea of having our own logo. There was no question in my mind that consumers would respond favorably to ours and would want to identify themselves as Liz customers. If we used it judiciously, it would enhance the reputation of the Liz Claiborne brand and become a symbol of everything the company stood for.

Liz had a very talented friend who owned a small graphic design firm. We hired him to come in and help us develop our identifying mark.

The logo we adopted in the end was a triangle with a line through it placed upward at an angle. The triangle represented our strength, and the line symbolized the company looking toward the future. Liz felt that the coloration, the triangle yellow and the line red, would work with any color garment we produced. But if necessary, we could always substitute different colors.

We wanted to be careful about using the logo and not overdo it. We put it on our t-shirts, sport shirts, our denims and other casual clothing. We didn't place it on our wear-to-work merchandise, as that seemed inappropriate for the office. Instead, on those kinds of items, we incorporated the logo as part of the label that went inside the garment.

The logo helped differentiate our merchandise from the competition, and consumers responded very well to it. Now, they would always know – and people looking at them would know – that they were wearing not just khaki pants but *Liz Claiborne* khaki pants and not just a polo shirt but a *Liz Claiborne* polo shirt.

Over time, our Liz Claiborne logo took its place with the most important symbols in the country, including Ralph Lauren's polo player and the distinctive swoosh that Nike was beginning to make famous.

During these early days of the company, the amounts of merchandize we produced were small, the sell-through was strong, and we had the opportunity to observe and learn as we went along. At some point, though, we started to understand that we might be onto something that could be very big.

I'll never forget one Saturday (we usually worked on Saturdays) we were sitting in our little showroom space merchandising one of the forthcoming lines, and the phone started to ring and ring and ring. It wouldn't stop. Finally Liz reluctantly went over and answered. It was a woman calling who said that she had just been shopping at Bloomingdale's on 59th street in New York. She was trying to buy a certain Liz Claiborne skirt, and she gave us the style number. She said "They're all out of it at Bloomingdale's, and I have to have the skirt. You've got to tell me where I can get it."

The woman was very insistent, and Liz didn't know how to handle her. She handed me the phone, and I listened to the woman tell the same story to me. I said "Some of the other Bloomingdale stores might have the skirt. Maybe the buyer or a salesperson at your store could find out if one of the other stores has it."

Her reply thrilled me. "They called all the stores. They couldn't find it. It's sold out. But I have to have that skirt!" There really wasn't much I could do, so I gave her the names of a couple other stores that were carrying our clothes and wished her well.

I remember the desperation in her voice like it was yesterday – how important it was for her to get that Liz Claiborne skirt. It was music to my ears!

That phone call wasn't the only sign:

Our Fall, 1977, line was just under way. We had a really nice 100% wool gabardine group on the line. As was the tradition then, we'd ship our fall goods to stores in the southwest in early June – earlier than most parts of the country. One of the first stores to get the group was Sanger Brothers in Dallas, Texas. The week after the goods were shipped, when I got in Monday morning, I called the buyer, introduced myself and asked her if our Fall merchandise had hit the floor.

She said that she was just going over the previous week's sales. Yes, our merchandise did hit and she had some good news: the downtown Sanger Harris store sold four skirts on the previous Saturday, which was a terrific number.

I said, "Wow isn't that great." We talked a little bit more and I asked her, "Do you think it's possible for you to go down to the floor and get some information on who bought the skirts? I just would like to have a feeling for who the customer is."

About an hour later she called me back and in a very excited voice told me about her little investigation. "I found the sales person who had sold those four skirts, and they were all sold to one customer!"

According to the salesperson, the customer was a young woman who had just graduated from law school and was beginning her professional career. She realized that she had absolutely nothing to wear for the office, and she had to start buying clothes that would make her look like a lawyer.

I can't tell you how excited this made me. Suddenly I felt I knew who our customer was, and more importantly, I knew we were riding a very strong wave, a demographic and societal shift that could take us very far. More women were going to law school. Women were looking for careers, starting to move to the workforce instead of staying at home. And they all needed to build their wardrobes for the office.

I remember picking up the phone and calling Art and Liz and giving them the news. I said to Liz, "This is our customer – this 25 year old woman who is going to work. She can't wear her school clothes any more. She needs an office wardrobe, and right now her closet is empty. This could be our opportunity."

And it was.

All across America, women were graduating from school and joining the workforce. But that's not the whole picture. At the same time, stay-at-home moms were emerging from their homes and going to work. Women were joining the professional ranks, becoming lawyers, accountants and teachers, and they were becoming bank tellers, restaurant maître d's and office supervisors of all kinds.

It was happening everywhere, and many of these women, especially in some of the smaller population centers, were realizing that they couldn't find the clothes they needed for their new occupations – until they found Liz Claiborne. For us it meant recognizing that we had something to offer them and figuring out how to reach them.

One town that that taught us and the retailers what we had going for us was Fargo, North Dakota. Fargo had a Dayton Company branch, but corporate headquarters in Minneapolis thought the market in Fargo was far too small and out of the way for Liz Claiborne merchandise.

I remember sitting with the merchandise manager and asking, "Why do you say that? Doesn't Fargo have school teachers? There's a university there – with professors! And professors' wives! They fit the Liz Claiborne profile perfectly. Don't think that because it's a small store in a small town that our clothes won't work there."

He came back at me. "Jerry, I want to tell you… have you ever been to Fargo?"

"No. Never."

"Well I have, and there's no way your merchandise will sell. These people wear jeans and boots. That's all they ever wear, all the time!"

I wouldn't accept that. "I don't believe it," I said.

He came back at me with a challenge. "I'll tell you what. We'll do an experiment. We'll put some of your goods in there. But when they've been sitting in the store for a month and nobody's bought anything, and I can't move them to any of my other stores, you'll take everything back from me."

I thought that was fair. "You got a deal," I replied.

We put together a very nice presentation of merchandise and shipped the goods to Fargo. They disappeared from the store almost immediately.

The merchandise manager called me about a week or so later. "Son of a gun," he said. "I didn't believe it. But you made a believer out of me."

It turned out that we had Liz Claiborne consumers everywhere. It didn't matter whether they lived in small towns, big cities, the north, the south, the Midwest or any place in between. Our merchandise worked for them. It was affordable, high quality, all-American clothing. And it was exactly right for the jobs they were going to. In fact I think we dressed half the teachers in this country.

Jan Sommers: Experiencing Liz as a Buyer

In 1980 Liz Claiborne was located at a chic "off the beaten track block" in the garment center, just far enough from the large buildings that housed most of the industry's sportswear firms. I was at the time a buyer for a small resident buying office servicing small, often family run department stores. Tasteful, trendy postcards were delivered to my buying office announcing Liz Claiborne's seasonal line openings and fashion shows, and I anticipated each opening as if it were the latest Broadway show. The colors of the card actually gave the hint of that season's color direction. I saved them all and posted them on the wall above my desk. The presentation was always given by Liz herself and modeled by real looking young women. The apparel was colorful and every item was sampled in 10-12 colors that made a dazzling display on a screen behind her as Liz announced each color. Fuchsia, Turquoise, (pronounced Tur-quaz), graphite, vicuna, lipstick, alabaster, citron, breen, even the color names were exciting!

Once the line was offered I would spend days sitting at the desk of Linda Larsen, a Liz Claiborne salesperson, which was available as she was spending long days showing the line. Occasionally Linda would run by to check her messages (no voicemail then) or have a bite of a sandwich. I would sit and write orders all day for small "Ma and Pa" stores from all around the country who had received my report heralding the new line and had given me the "open to buy" to write their orders for Liz Claiborne, the "hot" new fashion company. Little stores were stepping up and meeting $18,000 minimums (unheard of) to be able to represent the Liz "collection" in La

Crosse, Wisconsin, or Tuscaloosa, Alabama, or Salem, Oregon. This is when I met Jerry Chazen. He would come by and pat me on the back and say "keep writing" as he hurried past. I loved it.

Unfortunately, my little stores never received much of the line, as Saks Fifth Avenue and Lord and Taylor were using such huge quantities. Often, much of what did get shipped to my customers didn't match. Orders were shipped with tops without bottoms, jackets without coordinating skirts. Most of it sold anyway, but on one occasion I remember waiting on line to get into Jerry's office where I made my plea for a "return sticker" for Kay's Fashions in Kansas City, an account that was far from happy. As I stated my case to return 37 pieces of uncoordinated sportswear, Jerry smiled and said "you really care about your customers, don't you? You're pretty feisty when you need to be."

I made an impression and not too long after as the company grew and moved to brand new immaculate white showrooms with brick floors and beautiful displays I was asked to join the specialty store team.

It was a low man on the totem pole sales job but more exciting than anyone could have imagined. Now I got to see the line presented by Liz to an exclusive group of 10 individuals (mostly young working women ourselves), the sales force. We gave our feedback (only when asked), learned the lingo for each line – and we proudly became "Lizzies."

Our appeal extended into the Southern US, and we were able to reach consumers through many of the regional department store chains. One that was very important to us was Dillard's Department stores, headquartered in Little Rock, Arkansas.

I recently spoke with Bill Dillard, and we reflected on the early days of our business relationship, back in the early 1980s. Bill made some very kind comments about the effect we had on his business. "Liz Claiborne is certainly an important part of our history," he told me. "Because of Claiborne and later on a few other companies, we were able to drop the budget business and completely change the character of our stores."

Using the appeal of our merchandise, Bill moved Dillard's from low end to upscale offerings. And I'd like to think we played a small part in helping his company thrive and grow throughout the south and the southwest. We had a similar experience with another important department store group in the south called Belk's. We helped them create a much more updated group of stores, moving up from the lower price categories to becoming more like the large city stores such as Macy's and Marshall Field's.

Our merchandise was striking a chord with the American woman. She was clearly telling us how much she loved the group concept. We decided to expand it a bit by adding a special item once in a while that would coordinate with the group but also work with the clothes in her closet at home. We would take a heavier position in the item, and, because it was a single piece, we would expect a strong sell through, which would help to reduce the markdown percentage.

Most often the special item was a top, since our short history had already told us that tops outsold bottoms by a 2 to 1 and sometimes even 3 to 1. Consumers could be counted on because buying more than one top gave them additional outfits.

We started out with a blouse that Liz designed in a nylon fabric that had a very silky look and feel to it. Silk blouses at that time from designers like Anne Klein were selling for $100 or more, which probably relates to $500 today. Our blouses were in the $25 to $30 category.

Liz was particularly fond of blouses, and she liked designing them. When you think about it, a blouse is actually nothing more than the top of a dress, and that was in her DNA.

We put the special item blouse on the line in a variety of colors, and it became a best seller all over the country. Once we had that experience, Liz never stopped looking for special items.

Liz came up with the next special item, and it turned out to be in many ways the single most important one she ever designed. It propelled our company to a whole different level –

We were putting together the Fall, 1977 line. We weren't yet making any sweaters or any knitted goods. Instead, Liz decided to do a top in velour. Velour is a fabric very much like velvet except that it has a little more pile to it. Up until that time, I don't think it had ever been used in women's fashion apparel. It was mostly found in gowns and robes in the lingerie category. In fact, velour was a staple of the lingerie business. Most of the fabric that was manufactured in the United States came from one supplier, and most of that went to the lingerie makers. Some men's tops were also made in velour.

But Liz liked the idea of velour for women. She liked the way it felt and appreciated its casual look. Plus it was a little bit different. So she designed a top, and we put it into colors to coordinate with our fall collection. We bought some velour fabric, but not a lot, and made the top. Most of our retailers took some. I recall that Saks bought 36 pieces and decided to run an ad in the *New York Times* to show the top and also to introduce the Liz Claiborne line. I think the price was around $20 retail. It really was a tiny ad, and the top was only available at the 5th Avenue store.

The morning the ad ran, Ellen Daniel, the Saks buyer called. "I can't believe it! They're almost all gone. Ship me some more."

My reply made none of us happy: "We don't have anymore."

We had gotten our whole shipment of velour tops in and had shipped them all out to stores, all over the country. We weren't holding back. Saks got theirs and everybody else got theirs, and now we were out of them.

Ellen said, "That's impossible! You've got to get some more velour tops!"

I tried to give her some hope and replied, "Okay, let's see what we can do."

I called Art, gave him the update, and said "We've got to get some more velour. " I knew it wasn't a complicated garment and that we could make them quickly. But you can't make velour tops without velour. Art called our supplier, Burlington, but was told that all their machines were operating under deadline, busy making velour for next spring's lingerie orders. They couldn't help us.

We kept at it, though, and Art brought in the Burlington sales manager. We explained the whole situation to him, and I ended with, "There has to be something that you can do."

He thought for a moment and said, "We do have some velour we dyed for a customer, but it didn't meet their color standard. So the goods were put aside."

"What colors are we talking about?" Our own colors for that fall were Olive Green, Navy Blue, Black, Dark Red – earthy, autumn colors.

Our first big velour ad.

His answer wasn't what I expected. "We were working on next spring, so
we have peach and banana."

44

"Oh, my God," I thought, what are we going to do with those colors? We're talking about fall! Who's going to want peach and banana in the fall?"

But at the same time I was thinking, "Ok, what's more important? Having our velour tops in any color we can get, or not having any tops at all?

I said, "We want tops, so we'll take the goods."

It wasn't a lot of fabric, but we immediately put the tops into work in these strange colors and shipped them as soon as we they were finished. They went out to a lot of our customers, because what had happened at Saks with the original velour tops had happened everywhere – they had disappeared from the stores.

But we weren't done. We took everything Burlington had, but we needed more. The sales manager suggested we call the lingerie company that had rejected the peach and banana velour. Maybe they had some fabric they we not using.

I called the company, got the owner on the line, and we talked through the problem. "Do you have any fabric at all? Old fabric? Anything? We'll take it off your hands. We need velour."

The owner found some fabric for us, just a few thousand yards here and there. And again we shipped the fabric to the factory, made the tops as quickly as we could, shipped them to the stores, and they were gone – sold out.

It didn't take a genius to figure out that we were onto something with our velour clothing. No other women's company had ever designed with velour, and we had the category all to ourselves.

We followed up by going back to Burlington, who was really the sole supplier of this fabric and tying up their machinery. We wanted all the velour they could produce. Liz suggested that we make a small group of velour tops and also add a velour pant. She thought women would like it and would want to buy a top and a pant that went together – a velour outfit. In the next line we introduced our velour outfits. The retail response nationwide was almost beyond belief. It made our company.

A number of retail stores came in who felt that they could not sell the entire Liz collection but really wanted that velour group. We would not go along with that. I early on had instituted a rule in our showroom that stores had to buy our entire collection – they couldn't just pick out special items or special parts of the line. We inspected every order to make sure that the retailers were acting appropriately. The lesson to our customers was: If you're going to be a Liz Claiborne account, you had to order an appropriate amount of our goods. During all my years with the company we never varied from this philosophy. It wasn't a matter of arrogance; it just made good business sense.

(Fast forward twenty years. Another company decides to make a velour top and bottom, Liz having long ago ceasing manufacturing any such garments. The new company calls its velour top and pant outfit a tracksuit, and it becomes that firm's path to greatness. That company is Juicy Couture. And irony of ironies, Liz one day acquires Juicy.)

Things couldn't be going much better for our young company. Our Liz Claiborne merchandise was selling at full price with markdowns almost non-existent. Stores were running out and could hardly wait for the next group to come in. It was like that season after season after season.

Our growth was extraordinary: from $2 million in sales in 1976, to $7.4 million in 1977, to what seemed like an astounding $23.3 million in 1978.

We were a young, successful, growing company, and it seemed that everyone in the industry was interested in us. In early 1978, we were approached by a burgeoning specialty chain called The Limited. And at the time The Limited was a market-oriented company that was buying clothes from a whole variety of manufacturers mostly for the junior customer or the smaller missy customer. Leslie Wexner who was the owner and the head merchandiser at the time, knowing of our success, came to see us to explore whether there was some way The Limited and Liz Claiborne could do business together.

The Limited was capable of buying substantial quantities, and we liked the idea of having a specialty store customer to supplement our department store customers. So we began working with them. Since they catered to smaller women, they weren't interested in buying our usual run of sizes in any style, as they wanted to avoid the larger sizes found in a typical cutting. So we agreed to do special cuttings for them, which meant that they would have to see our upcoming line very early on, before we put anything into production. The merchandise we sold them did very well in their stores, and since they were expanding rapidly, their orders kept growing and growing.

Soon, though, the problems began.

When Liz started the designs for a new season, she focused on color – where she felt the consumer was moving. She would then select an appropriate palette of colors which would be incorporated into the new merchandise. Because of our longer production time, we had to make these decisions earlier than most of our competitors.

Liz's concept of color in each line, the way she put these colors together, and her take on what the important colors would be for upcoming seasons, were in many ways one of the biggest factors in our success.

As we worked with The Limited, we realized rather quickly that they were seemingly taking advantage of our color choices in other, non-Liz merchandise that they were either buying or producing themselves for their stores. This merchandise, reflecting our colors, was hitting the stores about the same time the Liz merchandise was. Obviously they had been privy to our upcoming color story and what we were doing for the new season months earlier.

It seemed to me that we were in an impossible situation, with one of our own customers actually competing with us and using our talent to their advantage. I felt that this situation made our company vulnerable and felt strongly that we stop selling to The Limited altogether.

Before taking any action, Liz, Art, Leonard and I met and discussed the problem. They were all very supportive of this course of action. We agreed that it didn't matter how much business we were doing with the account, we should stop working with them. The Limited at the time was our fourth or fifth largest account with every indication that that if we allowed them to continue buying from us, they would soon become our most important customer. Giving up a business of that size would be a major blow for most companies, but we were growing rapidly and were confident that there was sufficient department store demand to pick up the loss that we would experience when we cut The Limited loose.

We held a meeting with the people from The Limited and told them in the nicest way that we would complete all the orders that we had in the house, but we would not continue our relationship. The buyer and the merchandise manager were very disappointed and told us we were making a big mistake.

About two hours later, the phone rang and it was Leslie Wexner. "Are you crazy?" he exclaimed. "Are you really saying that you are refusing to sell to the best apparel specialty store in America?"

Leslie was terribly offended that we would have the chutzpah to say "You can't buy from us anymore." I told him the same thing I told his people, and I said, "Leslie, I know you're going to be successful. We'll go our way and you'll go your way and that will be it."

That happened around 30 years ago, and he has been annoyed about it ever since.

As I look back on that period, the transition away from having us as a supplier is probably what moved The Limited from a traditional market company to a vertical retailing. They certainly mastered it quickly and became enormously successful.

Despite our rapid growth, we were very careful in our forward planning. We were not kids on a roll but seasoned, experienced apparel people who knew that sometimes bad things happen that can trip you up. So while we planned for growth, we never overleveraged the company. We did not allow ourselves to get steamrollered by the stores to go beyond our financial capacity. For example, we would not put our money into manufacturing and delivering reorders. We liked the fact that we could sell out all of our planned production and leave it at that. We couldn't supply as much product as the stores would like, but so be it. We were more interested in investing in brand new merchandise, not reorders, and that became a vital part of our business model.

We were also very careful with our overhead. We were adding staff constantly to every part of the company, but we never got carried away. My own background had taught me that overhead should always follow sales, so we remained very prudent in the ways we invested in our expansion.

During these early flush times, the showroom became like an on-going party, a wonderful and exciting place to be. A kind of camaraderie developed between the department store buyers and our own salespeople, most of whom were ex-buyers. They all had war stories to tell, bosses to complain about and all kinds of news and gossip to exchange. Our sales people were charged with explaining and convincing the buyers that they had to buy everything on the line, that they didn't have anything to choose. They were good at it.

Karen Greenberg: My First Showroom Visit to Liz Claiborne

I remember it was the early 80's, and I was just promoted to the petite sportswear buyer at Dillard's department stores. This was a new department that I was going to launch for the store. My two key resources for the department were Liz Claiborne and Evan Picone.

Now I had been to a lot of showrooms as an assistant buyer and growing up in the industry, but the thought of walking into the Liz Claiborne showroom was quite intimidating. It had been less than 5 years since the first Liz Claiborne missy line was in department stores and it was quite the consumer hit. Now I had to build a strong Liz business for Dillard's in petites.

What took me by surprise and what made the Liz showroom different from the others was that it was more than just a showroom...it was an environment...people buzzing from booth to booth...lively...full of energy... even the color of the clothes added to the spirit. What I thought was going to be an intimidating experience ended up to be such a happy place to be. The people were not just sales people. They were as interested in the success of the business as I was. They would guide me in my placements. Total assortments were reviewed, with seasonality and geographic differences typically discussed. And although I was assigned a specific account executive, I got to know many of the Liz associates in the petite division. They were like family to each other...management knew all the buyers and addressed me at every market. I even got to know the buyer at Sanger Harris who was, at the time, my number one competitor!

Once you were in the showroom, all the competitive aspects of the business did not seem to matter. Everyone shared one common goal – regardless of your role on the wholesale side or the retail side or if you worked for Dillard's or Sanger Harris. Every person in that showroom wanted all involved to succeed.

The buyers themselves became part of the Liz phenomenon as the merchandise hit the floor and sold out. Many of the buyers who were involved with us in the early years shared our success in their own careers. They were fortunate enough to be part of our amazing growth and invariably had the best performance of any buyer in their respective stores, because the Liz merchandise sold so well. Their bosses, the merchandise managers, had a better performance record because of the tremendous gravitational pull of Liz Claiborne volume in their stores. Because the growth was so dramatic, a number of them became store presidents in those following years.

In those early years the problems we had were good problems to have. During our market weeks there were ongoing battles about which buyers would get the first appointments. There was a concern among the retailers that there wouldn't be enough product left for any store whose buyer didn't get in to see the line the first day it was open. Naturally, our sales people would try to get their buyers in first.

Our early successes had been astonishing, and I was loving every moment of it. But the pressure was starting to build on Liz and her very small staff. I think she felt like she was on a runaway train. She didn't say much to me about it, but her complaints and concerns got to me through Art.

I realized that we were working from early every morning to late every night doing all of the things that it took to run the company. I was so energized by what had been happening that I relished the hard work and couldn't wait to get to the office in the morning, and I didn't mind the late evenings. I was very concerned, though, about Liz's feelings and wanted to do everything necessary to maintain the spirit of camaraderie among the four of us.

My dreams for the company were just beginning to be realized, and I knew that in measuring our early success with the number of stores and consumers out there, that we could have unparalleled growth.

But it wasn't going to happen unless my partners were willing to participate in that dream. With Liz already unhappy with the challenges of a rapidly growing company, I knew that I had my work cut out for me in convincing them to buy into my dream.

We decided it would be best if the four partners spent some time talking about what we had accomplished and where we wanted to go next with the company. We needed to get together in a relaxed atmosphere, away from the frenzy of the showroom and the constantly ringing phones. So on a bright fall weekend in 1978, we headed to the Pocono Mountains and a little bed and breakfast where we could spend time together and talk about the future. Len and I brought our wives along with us.

We were all very excited about the progress of the company and the acceptance of our clothing line by the department stores and consumers. But now, with retailers starting to talk expansion, we had to start thinking in those terms as well. We were doing great, but now we had to grow. How would we do it? Who would do it? Beyond everything else, I wanted to push aside all the old fashioned garment business traditions that kept companies like ours small and struggling. There were very few fashion apparel manufacturers doing more than $10 or 15 million a year at the time. I wanted to go well beyond that.

We needed everyone to agree on a course of action. Did we want to stay small and continue on as we had – or did we want to swing for the fences? I wanted our new company to be a rocket. I wanted to take it to heights never before reached in our industry, and I was convinced we could do it. But first I had to convince my partners, and I knew that doing so would be my most important selling job.

We started the first session of our Poconos retreat at 8:00 Saturday morning. We even had lunch brought in. I let everyone know my feeling about growing the business in a big way. But Liz really didn't want it. She was becoming uncomfortable with not being able to oversee every part of our rapidly-expanding design operation. She was starting to feel that the business could get away from her. Leonard Boxer, our fourth partner, was pretty much in agreement with me. Art was having a real big problem because he always supported Liz's ideas, and going against the woman he loved would be extremely difficult for him. Yet I felt that he wanted the money and the life that a big, successful company would bring to him and Liz. He and I never talked about it, but subsequent events would prove me right.

We talked and we talked – about what we had accomplished in a very short time and how we had pulled it off. We talked about what was happening in retail, what the trends were, how we could fit in, how we could do it. We talked until 6:00 that evening, when we stopped for dinner, promising that we would return the next day and reach a conclusion. Simona and Anita rejoined the group, and we had a lovely evening together.

Sunday morning we were right back at it. Immediately I saw that Liz and Art were starting to move toward my point of view. There were things Liz liked about what was happening – she was becoming an important person. Even though she was shy and hadn't wished for fame and fortune, she did enjoy many things about her new life.

At one point on that Sunday morning we were talking about all the customers who were now wearing Liz's clothes. I said, "Look at what you're doing for these women. Why not keep doing it for them? They're happy with you. Hey, they love you! You're making all of these wonderful clothes for them. This is our opportunity to turn this company into a phenomenon."

We knew that we were taking care of women entering the workforce. So I said, "I promise you something Liz. When they write the history of this period – how women are not staying home any more but are heading into the offices and businesses all over the country and how it all started and what became of it – one of those pages is going to have a footnote, and the footnote is going to say, 'The designer most responsible for dressing these women was Liz Claiborne.'"

Everybody laughed. Liz laughed. And I said "Liz, I've never been more serious in my life." I meant it, and I was right.

In the end, everyone bought in. And we left the Poconos ready to grow.

One of the first barriers to growth was our inability to fill all of the orders we were receiving. Invariably, we would end up shipping less merchandise to the stores then they wanted. That was especially true with our best styles and colors. We simply couldn't find enough production capacity in the US to meet the demand – a problem that would soon lead us to Asia in search of factories that could make our goods in the quantity, and with the quality, that we needed.

Looking to Asia for manufacturing help was at the very least unusual and something that no fashion company had yet done. But as we'll see in the next chapter, it may have been the best thing that ever happened to Liz Claiborne, Inc.

Fun Time — taken at my daughter Louise's wedding. — Liz, Leonard, Jerry, Art

In time, the dreams I dreamed at our Poconos retreat became a reality. We could have remained a tiny company, but we didn't. We became a giant, the biggest fashion company the world had ever seen.

How we did it, of course, is the rest of the story. It didn't just happen. It wasn't magic.

Part of the story was the big demographic wave and the dramatic trends we were riding: the size of the boomer generation; women entering the work force by the tens of thousands; the beginning of the tremendous expansion of department stores; the rise of the malls suddenly being built all over the country.

We were in the right place at the right time. There's no doubt about that. Yet, as people have pointed out to me, we were not the only company making clothes for that consumer. There were a lot of companies competing with us. So how did Liz Claiborne get so big in the face of literally hundreds of firms trying to do the same thing?

We had other vitally important things going for us: we had the right people with the right talent and the right vision. We were willing to break the rules

– especially the hard and fast marketing rules of the fashion industry. We were willing to try new things. We planned and choreographed every move. We worked hard. And of course we found that the old saying was true: "The harder you work, the luckier you get."

Chapter 3

Blazing the Trail to Global Production

Four times each year, we would sit down and come up with our sales budget for the forthcoming season. We were growing too fast to rely on what we did the same season the year before. Instead, we had to take into account the momentum of the business. Because of my retail background, I believed in bottom-up planning: Figure out how much could we sell to each of our customers, add it all up and decide on a sensible budget for the new season.

As we grew, talking about an individual customer – Macy's, Bloomingdale's, etc. – was not fundamental enough. We had to focus on how much we could sell in each of the doors we were in for each of those customers. The dollar figures we came up with would then have to be translated into specific merchandise – "How many blouses? How many skirts?" – for each item we intended to sell.

The design team would then make it all happen. As we got larger and the dollars and quantities of goods grew, the budget process became more and more important, but that came later. In 1978, we had a different kind of problem. As we were sitting down and discussing our budgets for 1979, we were stymied by the lack of production facilities available to us.

The four of us tried to have dinner almost every night to discuss business, as each of us was too busy during the day. At one of these dinners, Leonard shared with us his concern over finding additional contractors to handle our product. We could only go to union shops and, frankly, there weren't enough of them capable of making merchandise at our quality level. We kicked a lot of ideas around, including trying to find nonunion shops that we could use. As the conversation moved on and I thought about my own background working with foreign suppliers, I suggested that we might want to try looking to Asian sources for help.

Liz's reaction was swift and impassioned. "Never!" she exclaimed.

She went on, "We can't even supervise the factories we're using in New Jersey and Pennsylvania! How can we possibly control work that's being done 10,000 miles away?"

I suppose I shouldn't have been surprised. As the only one of the four of us with experience producing garments overseas, my comfort level with the idea was pretty high. I felt strongly that we could control the situation, and that we could get the quantity and the quality we wanted –at a significant savings over our current US production.

We went on trying to find additional factories in the US, but our attempts met with failure. The unions were not at all helpful in the effort.

Chinese Factory – Jerry with manager.

We identified a company in Taiwan that was making blouses for some

European manufacturers and had a good reputation. We went over our production concerns again with Liz, and Leonard suggested that we could do a test and evaluate the results. We put a small quantity of one blouse into a factory in Taiwan. It was a relatively difficult, complicated style. In fact, we had not been able to find a factory in the States that could sew this blouse properly. Some weeks later that first lot arrived by air in our offices, and Liz was blown away. It was nicer than anything we had done domestically, and it cost far less than what we had been paying.

That blouse opened the door, and we walked through it. Actually Leonard walked through it and went on to establish our network of Asian production facilities.

He found a factory in South Korea that was making men's wool suits for an English retailer. He figured that if they could make quality men's suits, they certainly could make ladies jackets, pants, and skirts. He was right. They did a beautiful job for us, and, encouraged by the results, he looked for and found other factories for our other types of merchandise. Leonard became a virtual commuter to Asia, flying to Hong Kong, South Korea, and Taiwan to find more factories we could contract with.

The good news is that the factory owners were smart, entrepreneurial and would go out of their way to make sure we were properly taken care of. The bad news is that despite everyone's willingness, the complications for us were enormous.

We were still using domestic fabrics, so we had to send our fabrics overseas. We had to work with the factories to make sure that they did the job right with these fabrics we were sending them. And then of course we had to arrange to bring the finished goods back to the US. There were all sorts of rules and regulations in customs that we had to learn about at the beginning. There were duties that had to be paid on the garments we brought into the US. And in the early days we had to deal with quotas that the US government had set up to protect the domestic garment industry.

Naturally, our early experiences overseas involved a lot of trial and error, but as I said, all the manufacturers we dealt with were extremely hardworking, ethical, and smart. The manufacturing community in Taiwan was made up of people who had fled China during the Cultural Revolution and were rebuilding their lives in their new country. They were educated, not necessarily able to speak English, but they caught on quickly enough. The same was true in Hong Kong. Back then Hong Kong was almost a third world country but was progressing very quickly. The Chinese families there were also for the most part refugees of the Cultural Revolution and determined to make new lives for themselves. They wanted to do business wherever and with whomever they could. European manufacturers, the British in particular, were much faster getting involved with them than we in the States were.

Because we were still in the Cold War and our country had a strained relationship with China, we could not manufacture anything there. In fact, we had to be very careful to make sure the merchandise we were ordering was not being made in China and then transferred to Hong Kong for finishing.

Meanwhile in New York, a lot of discussion was taking place about the possible effect that the foreign labels might have on the sale of our merchandise. US law mandated that the country of manufacture be prominently displayed on a label in the back center of the garment. We worried about whether our consumer would consider clothing made in Hong Kong, or South Korea, or Taiwan to be of lesser quality than what they were used to. I did as much testing as I could in the showroom, asking people what their feelings were about the label issue, and by and large they didn't seem to care.

When the first of our Asian-manufactured merchandise got to the selling floor, we held our collective breath. But everything was fine – there was no problem at all. As a matter of fact the remarks we got back from consumers were complimentary because people were noticing how well made these garments were.

Little by little we took all of our production overseas. Soon it made sense for us to begin buying fabric overseas as well. It was much easier for the Asian factories to use goods made in Asia than to send the fabric over from the US. The textile industry in Asia and particularly in Japan had grown up while no one – in the US at least – was looking. They now were equipped with the most modern machinery, a dedicated workforce, and terrific processes for achieving a high level of quality in their work.

Without going into a lot of detail, it should be noted for the record that almost all of the other production functions that were initially being done in the States were moved to Asia, including sample making. All of the findings for our garments (zippers, belts, buttons, and the like) also began to be made in Asia as well.

All of our overseas manufacturing was helped tremendously by developments in technology that allowed certain vital functions that had been done by hand for centuries to be computerized. One of the most important related to pattern grading – the way a pattern had to be changed proportionally to fit the entire range of sizes we wanted to manufacture. This and other technological innovations were having a big impact on the industry, creating time and cost savings, and they were all available to us through our Asian manufacturers.

In retrospect, if I were asked to identify the one thing that was primarily responsible for the financial success of Liz Claiborne, I would say it was the movement of our production to Asia and the development of our overseas supplier structure.

While the building of our overseas organization was largely in Leonard's hands, Art did get involved with a lot of the personnel issues involved with setting up the people who would work for us in these countries and be responsible for monitoring production in the various factories making garments for us. Also, Liz and Art would make periodic trips to Asia to show our people, the manufacturers and the suppliers that we cared about them and to use her eye to make sure everything was going well.

We eventually opened an office in Hong Kong to oversee all production in Asia. The office grew from thirteen people in 1981 to eventually number 1000 employees.

Our production people in the States would travel overseas on a regular basis to work with the groups we were doing business with. They would go into the factories to instruct employees on quality and would work with the local supplier community to improve their standards. We wanted to deliver a product that we were proud of, and we did everything we could to make sure of it.

There's no question that we owed a lot of our success to our overseas employees. We decided early on that we did not want to populate our offices overseas with ex-pats – Americans sent over to live in the Asian country and work for us. Moving people overseas was a very expensive proposition, since any salary package for Americans would have to include all sorts of perks, including company-provided living quarters, a food allowance, and numerous benefits.

Instead, we felt that there were qualified locals in all these countries who we could train and bring back to the States to teach them about Liz Claiborne, our culture, how we work and our priorities. We also wanted them to meet our domestic employees so everyone would get comfortable with everyone else. That's the approach we took, and we did not regret it. We never had more than a small handful of Americans working for us overseas, no matter how big we got. By far the vast majority of our employees were native to the areas in which we were doing business. These folks did a great job. They became real "Lizzies" and believed in the company and the culture of the company.

We began moving into foreign production in early 1979. By 1980, half of our garments were produced overseas. And by 1982, we were no longer making anything at all in the United States.

Through the change, we continued to stay true to our mission of affordable designer looks at reasonable prices, while keeping the quality high. We stayed the course even as we were creating increasing amounts, even enormous amounts, of merchandise. We were able to stick to our price and quality goals only because we had so many factories to choose from overseas. If we hadn't moved our production, I am convinced that there never could have been a Liz Claiborne as we know it – never.

Of course the other side of this equation made no one happy. No one, least of all me, wanted to see work taken away from American companies. But the truth was that we had no choice: There was no way that the United States had the labor available or the factory capacity to manufacture the amount of product that we needed. And even though the unions opposed our moves and fought with us constantly, they knew that if we did an about face and said "Ok, we'll move our entire production back to the States," there would be no place to move it. And the sad truth is that there still isn't.

The factories serving the garment industry in our country operated for years under a false sense of security that developed because of protectionism. The theory was that since companies like Liz were using cheap overseas labor, the government would charge duty when we brought the garments into the country in order to equalize costs. We'd have to charge more to our customers, making the playing field even with our competitors who were producing their goods in the US. In addition, there were bilateral agreements between the major exporting countries and the United States imposing quotas that limited the amount of certain types of merchandise that could be imported into the US. In these ways our government thought it was doing a good job of protecting domestic industry.

These efforts eventually did more harm than good for the people and companies the government was trying to protect. The industry didn't have to compete as vigorously as it should have. It didn't strive to stay up to date, make capital investments for new equipment or innovate.

But that's exactly what was happening in other parts of the world – they were building factories that were much more efficient, produced more and better products, faster, more cheaply, and with much better quality than we could in the US.

With Liz and later on other companies producing garments overseas, some textile mills in the US started to feel the crunch. There was of course a bitter outcry from unions and politicians. At times *Women's Wear Daily* would run stories about a textile factory in, say, a small town in South Carolina closing and throwing fifty or sixty people out of work. What *Women's Wear* didn't say was that very often the factory in question had been built sometime in the 19th century and hadn't changed since. It still had the same old antiquated looms and other equipment that had been installed 100 years ago, with inefficient manufacturing processes to match. The owners hadn't tried to modernize and compete. They didn't think they needed to because they were protected, and whatever they could make, they could sell.

Much of what I felt at the time was wrapped up in a speech I made in 1990 to a convention of 250 American textile executives. I was trying to get them to understand that if they wanted to stay in the textile business they had to start thinking about how they could compete in global markets. With manufacturing moving overseas, apparel companies would find it necessary to buy their fabric overseas, just as we had at Liz Claiborne. These textile people had to understand that textile manufacturing had to be close to the sewing machines. Most of these executives had never even traveled overseas to Asia to look at their competition.

The global marketplace that has since developed make those old words of mine sound prophetic. Just look at the business headline in today's newspaper: in the first quarter of 2010 General Motors *produced* and sold more cars in China than they did in the US! Without the Chinese market, there certainly wouldn't be a General Motors today. Like GM, our textile manufacturers should have taken their skills and moved with them overseas years ago. To my knowledge not a single US manufacturer ever did.

There is no question that garment manufacturing's contribution to the growth of our country has been immeasurable. It's too bad that well-intentioned but destructive laws have done their part in hurting the industry so badly. Throughout the last century, waves of immigrants from different countries came to work in the factories, helping to build the companies and the national economy. In the process, they bootstrapped themselves to the middle class and beyond.

In most cases, the children of the garment workers did not want to follow in their parents' footsteps and become garment workers themselves. They went to school and followed the American dream to a better life. The same holds true today. Right now in the New York area, the garment workers are primarily first generation Chinese immigrants. Many can't speak English, but their kids can go to great public schools like Stuyvesant High School and Bronx High School of Science and then on to the best universities. And then, they're out of the garment world.

The positive impact of the garment business isn't just a US phenomenon. National economies grow and upward mobility takes place all over the world because of this industry. Production and competition lifts everyone.

When we opened our first office in Hong Kong, the employees there worked for probably 10% of the pay that we were giving people in the US, and we are talking about skilled office workers. Today in Hong Kong, only 30 years later, the wage rates are comparable to New York City.

Hong Kong is now a thriving economy and has become one of the most expensive cities to live in the world. The cost of clothing is comparable to the US. Those of us who follow the industry know that every important European and American design company has a retail presence there. There are million-dollar apartments there just as in the United States.

The fact that Hong Kong quickly went from "emerging nation" status to equal standing with major cities of the world in such a short period of time is a lesson for all of us in the power of global trade.

The same thing has happened in other Asian countries as well. Taiwan, South Korea, and Hong Kong have advanced so far that, while once almost 100 percent of our manufacturing was done in these countries, now we do little or none. The fact is that as their economies grew, so did the cost of labor, to the point that they are now noncompetitive with other parts of Asia. The labor market has moved on to less developed countries like Sri Lanka, Thailand, Indonesia, but most especially China.

As business has flooded into China, its economy has grown so quickly and to such an extent that its once "inexhaustible labor force" is demanding higher wages. The garment industry finds itself competing for labor with better-paying industries, including electronics and construction among others. Growth has been so rapid that economists now speculate on how much longer it will take until China passes the US in various aspects of its economy. I think it is thrilling that these changes have taken place during my time in the garment industry. When we started to produce merchandise in China, no one could have predicted how quickly all this would happen – or that it would happen at all.

I was and still am a big believer in free trade in a global economy. And I think that we're much closer to it than when we started our company. Perhaps in the next 50 or 100 years we will have a free trade economy world-wide. It will happen as more and more emerging nations follow in the footsteps of the countries I have been discussing and become more and more self-sufficient, start to compete, and begin to see their wages rise up closer to the levels of more developed countries.

As a matter of fact, in a recent issue of *Forbes* magazine, the cover story was about how now is the time to start investing in Africa – don't let the opportunity pass you by.

I am such a believer in the power of free trade to improve the world that my first large philanthropic gift was to Columbia University for an institute to study and foster business in a borderless world. But I'll save that story for later in the book.

We definitely broke a rule of business when we took our manufacturing overseas. We were virtually the only company in our price category doing it. We knew that we had a short-term head start on the rest of the industry, that we would soon be copied by people who would see the quality of the product that we were shipping and decide that they better join the movement.

The unions were unhappy. But they couldn't do anything about it – they couldn't stop us. Their contract, however, allowed them to collect "compensatory damages" from us based on the amount of goods we were manufacturing overseas. The logic was that we had to make up for the benefit and pension programs of the union workers that were not being funded by the overseas manufacturers, so we had to pay in directly.

We didn't quite understand this since all of our domestic employees, and we had hundreds back then, still doing all of our pattern making, sample making, shipping, and so on. They were union members, and we were paying into a pension and benefits package for all of them.

At any rate, we were forced to go along with the union's demands since, according to our attorneys, we had no choice. If we didn't pay, it would represent a default in our union contract, and we would be subject to a strike. We certainly didn't want that to happen. So at the end of each year we would sit down and have settlement meetings with the union, their attorneys, and our attorneys. We would come up with a figure that would satisfy them – or come close at least – while still being something we could afford to pay without harming the company.

Going overseas with production solved a lot of problems for us, but it also created new sales and marketing challenges. As we moved our production, Liz Claiborne merchandise had to be ordered at least 6 months before we could expect to ship the garments to our customers. It took a long time to order the textiles, have proper samples made, and do all of the color matching and coordinating that was necessary for a line like ours. Then the merchandise had to be made and put on a cargo ship for an excruciatingly slow 30 to 45 day voyage to the US. All that time had to be factored in. It meant that we had to plan production months before the buyers would see the new line or place any orders. It became a constant struggle to produce the right amount of garments in the right sizes and colors before we knew what the buyers' reactions would be to the line.

Many very important decisions went into planning our production and issuing a cutting ticket: How many units of a particular style did we want to manufacture? How many units of each color in that style did we want to put into work? Such basic decisions had to be made with every single one of the styles that we had on our line – that meant hundreds and eventually thousands of styles each season. And we had five seasons a year!

Other manufacturers, still producing their goods domestically, had a much shorter lead time and could produce samples, market their lines to the retailers, collect their orders and *then* issue their cutting tickets. They knew what they were dealing with in terms of demand.

Well, we did not have that luxury.

As our salespeople worked with the retail buyers, they had the very difficult job of making sure that the orders being written corresponded to our reality: we had already placed our manufacturing orders, and they were difficult if not impossible to change.

We did what we could in the showroom to put the buyers on the right track. The most efficient technique for us was to explain to the buyers that if they wanted to get good delivery on the new line, it was important that they buy it pretty much the same way that we owned it.

That sounded great but it didn't always work. We had to come up with other techniques to deal with the problem.

Jan Sommers: Selling It the Way We Owned It

After Liz's fashion presentation Jerry would go through the line style by style sharing our ownership quantities and making sure we understood the importance of selling the line the way we owned it. Our pricing, fabrics, and quality were a result of production in Asia and thus commitments had been made way before our first buyer came to town. A good seller sold to ownership, not to personal preference or creative combinations. If the line was not sold correctly chances were your account would not get the presentation and Liz's message onto to the selling floor. It was a unique talent, because Liz and the production team were not always right, and sometimes the retailer saw opportunities in colors or styles we did not own enough of.

We became almost cultish in our belief that we were serving the masses of women coming out of college and into the workforce. These hippie girls had spent their college days in flannel shirts and dungarees! They needed our help! We also proudly said "mothers and daughters shop together for Liz Claiborne." It was true. Liz knew no age.

We worked hard, often to 9 or 9:30 PM. We had hundreds of accounts on waiting lists to buy the line and we felt privileged to be there. Once the orders came in we had to analyze them, make sure they were balanced and represented the line correctly as Liz saw it and Jerry taught us.

Unfortunately even after we cajoled our customers into writing a good representation of the line we still had issues with oversold and undersold product. Jerry and his right hand young marketing director, Mitchell Lewis, decided to have a campaign called "Operation Switch." It was our job to switch the customers who had written Blue/green color stories into pink/ orange color stories! Soon after it was part of every sales season's post mortem. It became known as Op Switch. It was dreaded by all.

Op Switch was successful to a certain degree. It did encourage stores to be more adventurous in trying new style directions and not just boring interpretations of an exciting collection. And it did indeed increase the shipping percentage.

Unfortunately, the shipping percentage still rarely got above 60-65% in the specialty store division, and it was a daily source of stress for customers and specialty store sales exec's. We were demanding collections but shipping pieces!

One day Jerry called the Specialty Store Sales team (there were four of us) into his office. He said "I have an idea. What if your stores, the little guys, were guaranteed 95-100% of their order if they wrote it exactly as we wanted in a pre-determined selection? We could call it a "module," and it would be planned and produced in advance. Units and fabrics would be planned and purchased separately for these orders.

At first we were excited and then cautious. Would our accounts do it? Would they buy short skirts if they sold long? Double breasted jackets when they wanted single breasted. Linen when they wanted silk?

Would they resent their own lack of creativity? Would we appear arrogant?

The first season we planned 50 modules and carefully explained the new plan to protect and service specialty stores. Most were suspicious, some tried it. We sold out of modules in a week!

Without sounding arrogant we tried to explain to our customers how difficult it was to supply them properly without cooperation on their part.

March 6, 1989

Dear LIZ CLAIBORNE Customer:

The untimely receipt of orders makes it extremely difficult for us to service you as well as we would like to. The continuing growth of our business together and the greater pressure on sources of supply this year dictates that we make the following requests of you:

1. To protect your on-order it is strongly recommended that orders be placed as quickly as possible. Please make every effect to place your order one week after your working appointment. The sooner we receive your order the faster we can attempt to make any possible adjustment in our ownership to accommodate your individual needs.

2. In addition to submitting your order on a timely basis, please make every effort to use the included color codes when writing up your orders. For your convenience they have been listed on the descriptive list beside their respective colors.

3. Consequently, orders received later than two weeks after your working appointment run a high risk of resulting in substantial deletions.

4. Our ownership ratios have been worked out over the months of planning and are consistent with our most current retail experience. Plan your assortments as closely as possible to the percentage recommended by your account executive. Overemphasizing one group at the expense of others inevitably causes delays in the flow of goods since we plan our shipping rotations on a group by group basis to insure constant newness on your selling floor.

We would like to thank you in advance for helping us service you better by implementing the above suggestions. We are sure it will be mutually advantageous.

Liz Claiborne, Inc.

The program was a huge success and soon we were selling hundreds every season. Those group presentations became module presentations. I would show every piece of a merchandise group and then edit it for all to see what their store module included. They were pleased to see our selections for them and thrilled to be guaranteed delivery. Jerry's vision was a success.

———

The system in the showroom was that the buyers would sit and block out the line and then typically take their order pads back to their home office and write the orders. We would wait several weeks before enough orders came in so that we could see what we were dealing with and begin to anticipate what problems we would have in delivery.

With all of that work, all of the trials and tribulations, and even though we would typically oversell our total production, we would still get stuck with goods at the end. Occasionally it would be a problem of getting the colors wrong. Or every once in awhile the buyers would say "We just don't like that style," and wouldn't buy anything close to the amount of merchandise that we had actually put in work. And of course no matter how carefully we tried to avoid it, there would be odds and ends in certain styles or colors that we couldn't ship. At our volume of business, "odds and ends" could mean hundreds or sometimes thousands of units.

In the old days, retailers might come to the manufacturers at the end of a season, buy up the discontinued items or broken sizes at a reduced price, and run a big sale. But that didn't work for us because we were constantly shipping new merchandise into the stores and didn't want to see last season's items in a big sale competing against our new line. What we wanted was for the stores to take their markdowns at the end of a season and just get rid of the excess merchandise.

This of course left us with the problem of what to do with our leftovers. There were then and are now retail organizations that buy manufacturers' closeouts. Some of the most well-known of these off-price retailers today are Loehmann's, TJ Maxx, Marshall's, and Ross Stores. We did have our share of closeouts and managed to get rid of them to these traditional off-price buyers.

But the handwriting was on the wall. As the company got bigger, we realized that even if we kept our percentage of closeouts to a reasonable level, there were probably more garments than these retailers could absorb.

Eventually, though, the problem of what to do with this merchandise turned into a great opportunity, and a new kind of store and shopping experience came into being: the outlet mall.

After we had been in business for a few years, I was visited one day by a man named Stanley Tanger. Stanley had a men's shirt manufacturing business in Connecticut and was faced with the problem of what to do with his own excess goods. He had come up with the idea of opening a store where he could sell just his own leftover merchandise and no one else's. But he took the idea a lot farther – he wanted to create a whole center of many stores, with each one devoted to just one manufacturer, where they would offer their closeout merchandise to the public. The center would be located a distance from the metropolitan areas where the department stores were located. In that way, it would not be viewed as competitive.

I thought about his idea, and I thought about our problem, and I decided I liked what I was hearing. I felt that our own outlet store would give us better control of our closeout merchandise. The way things were now, once we sold our closeouts to the off-price retailers, we had no control over what they did with it, how the merchandise was shown. We were very concerned about what harm that could be doing to our label. But being able to sell the excess in our own stores, with our own people, under conditions we could totally control, sounded like a great idea.

In addition, I was completely certain that the amount of excess inventory would grow as our volume grew, mainly because, as I explained earlier, of the enormous lead time we needed to produce our goods overseas.

I told Stanley that we were very interested in his idea, and that as soon as he got further along with his plans, he should contact us. He did, and eventually we became a tenant in one of his first centers in Kittery, Maine. We followed up rather quickly with a second center in North Conway, New Hampshire. Both of these centers were in resort regions of their states, far away from any of our full-price customers. In fact, this became a strategy: over the years we positioned many of our outlet stores in resort areas.

I spoke earlier about my friend Alan Glen from the University of Wisconsin. He was responsible for getting me into the fashion industry in the first place.

. Alan himself had left the apparel business and had become a real estate developer in Washington D.C. We were still close friends, and I called Alan and told him about our company's needs for additional outlet stores.

I said, "Alan, I think this could be a terrific business for you. I think these outlet centers are going to become very, very important to the industry."

I was anticipating huge increases in close-out merchandise across the industry as more and more manufacturers followed us overseas and were forced to put garments into work, as we had been doing, long before getting orders from the retailers. It was obvious to me that if we were having these problems, everybody was going to be having them.

I explained the situation to Alan, and he caught on immediately.

I went further, "If you could find appropriate locations that wouldn't interfere with the department stores, we and other manufacturers could have a place to put our excess merchandise."

Alan loved the idea, and he and his business partner, Cheryl McArthur, started to look for locations. We gave them some guidelines as to how many miles away from a metropolitan area the location had to be. The idea was that the department store customer would have to go out of her way to get to the center. That way, we wouldn't be taking business away from the department stores, who were still going to be our most important customers. Alan would have to figure in travel time and route options: the outlet centers not only had to be located away from cities, but they had to be accessible via good highways so they could be reached without any real difficulty.

I discussed this new version of retailing with the board. We even discussed the possibility of investing in Alan and Cheryl's business, which came to be called McArthur / Glen and was to become a major player in the designer outlet business. By the time they merged with another outlet company in the 1990s, they had grown to 19 outlet centers. Unfortunately, the board wanted no part of it.

Because we had come to Alan with the idea, and because of the strength of our name in the marketplace, we were given "most favored nation" treatment, becoming the anchor tenant and getting our choice of location in the centers. We hired an executive named Jeff Schendel to be our outlet guru, and he worked very closely with the developers and their people in determining whether a particular location was right for us.

We developed these stores very, very quietly. The department stores were obviously nervous about this new phenomenon. Frankly, they felt that we were doing a terrible thing to them that would destroy their business. It was our job to calm them down and explain why we felt the outlet centers would not hurt them. We needed them to understand why we had to have places under our control where we could sell off our excess merchandise under conditions that would not denigrate the label. Ultimately it was a matter of – "well, let's see what happens."

The outlet centers were built, the consumer responded, and the stores became a huge success. The customers proved willing to buy these leftover items – sometimes in very strange colors or styles. And we ended up getting a better price for our merchandise than we had been getting from the traditional off-price buyers.

Because we were so careful in choosing locations for these outlets, their success didn't seem to affect our business in the department stores one single bit. Over the years, as Liz Claiborne grew, our need for a way to dispose of excess merchandise grew, and we continued to work with developers to open up locations all across the country.

In 1985 our volume at these outlets was $3.9 million, and by 1989 it had grown to $32.9 million. One year later we doubled to $62 million, and in another two years – 1992 – we almost doubled again, to $114 million in sales. In 1996 we hit $194 million.

In time we even started to produce goods especially for the outlet stores. The clothes might be slightly different from what was in our regular line. Manufacturing these special goods helped the outlet business because we made them in a range of sizes that we knew was right for our consumers. In contrast, the excess clothing that we sent to the outlets would often be in odd "leftover" sizes that not too many people would be happy with. We also at times had extra fabric we had no use for, so we'd make up some garments with it and ship to the outlets.

The whole huge outlet center industry grew beyond anyone's expectations. The traditional closeout retailers like TJ Maxx, Marshall's, and Ross Stores grew rapidly as well. Eventually even I have to admit that the business got so big that there must have been some effect on department store sales. To some degree, I think it also contributed to the constant sale atmosphere that developed in most of the department stores, and which, as we'll see later, ended up hurting everyone.

Chapter 4

Breaking the Marketing Rules

Liz Claiborne succeeded in great measure because of our willingness to break the rules of the apparel industry. Wherever we saw a better way, we took it. For the most part we convinced our business partners and customers to go along for the ride. Everyone benefited, most of all the consumer, who was given a new and better shopping experience. Our success at breaking the rules motivated our competitors to copy many of the innovations we pioneered. They say that imitation is the sincerest form of flattery, and I can say that as I look over the positive changes that took place in the industry in the last 30 years, I feel very, very flattered.

To outsiders, and perhaps even to the younger people in the fashion industry, it probably doesn't sound like much – but one of the greatest breakthroughs we ever engineered was to convince the big retailers to give Liz its own department number.

Readers may need a bit of background on the state of the retail business back in the 1970s in order to understand the significance of this change.

The department stores were set up by classification: a blouse department, a pant department, a jacket department, a sweater department, and so on. I discussed in Chapter 3 how we were able to persuade retailers to keep the Liz line together in one place. The usual practice would have been to take each item out and stick it in a department with like items – Liz blouses with all the other blouses the store was selling, Liz jackets with all of the stores' jackets, etc.

Simona & Mike Hecht – CEO of Broadway L.A.

But we wanted our customers to experience the line in its entirety so they could pick out coordinated items for their wardrobe. This was the way we conceived of each collection and the way Liz designed it.

The stores went along, the idea worked, and our clothing sold well.

We used our showroom to reinforce the idea that we were showing designer clothes at affordable prices. Our showroom itself had to give the impression that the buyers were looking at something special.

Karen Greenberg: My First Market as a Liz Claiborne Employee

All account executive had the seasonal books with style numbers and pictures to help learn the line. We sat as if we were attending a fashion show and waited for Liz herself to take us through the lines from concept to color, fabric, silhouette and to tell us why each piece made the line. Her presentation would give us all the things we needed to know in order to truly understand the line before selling it to our buyers.

Then we practiced...literally seven days of learning all aspects of the line to make sure we were prepared. There was a lot of show and tell, memorizing – it was like being back in school again. Now I realized why I was so impressed as a buyer when I shopped the line. The prep, the practice....this company treated market like a Broadway show. And you are an understudy literally until you are ready to perform yourself.

Liz Claiborne had built such a great reputation in the marketplace for its product and its people that each of us had to strive to live up to the name. The company used to say it is the ultimate consumer who will tell us if we are right or wrong, not the buyer. But we had to get the product past the buyer so that the consumer could judge.

I remember my first market. There were maybe two or three sample lines in the showroom. Each account executive had a booth that we basically worked in all day. It was the account executive who did all the walking and hanging and displaying of product for each grouping. We literally would sit with our account and write different assortments for the A volume stores versus the D-E-F volume stores.

We would hang and un-hang outfits and then walk them back to the stationary place where they lived for market week. I remember our showroom had a step up from where the samples were kept to the working booth. The coordination of high heels, managing the step and holding the product was a balancing act. Every now and then you would hear "kaboom" which meant one account executive missed the step. It was a sound that became well known in the showroom.

Samples were treated with the utmost respect. If someone was dragging a sample or carrying it too low to the ground where it could get dirty you would hear someone say, "You are dragging your paycheck." To this day, I use that Liz'ism, which is an affectionate way of referring to our business principles.

No Gum in the Showroom!

I remember the time I was in the showroom working with my account and Mr Chazen walked by and put my hand out in front of my mouth. I was chewing gum, and he literally had me take it out of my mouth and put it in his hand. I was scared to death, but he explained ever so kindly, "We don't chew gum in the showroom." And to this day, I don't. It really is unprofessional. How do you talk and chew at the same time? Rude!

Then we started thinking that there might be more we could do, and here our knowledge of how stores planned, budgeted, and bought inventory came into play. Since we had our own location in the stores, and since our merchandise was not mixed in with any other manufacturers', it seemed to me that we should have our own department number. This would mean a lot more than just having the Liz name on a wall or hanging over a rack of merchandise. It would be a huge departure from the way business had been done for decades. In fact, it was unheard of.

Burt Tansky, Helen Galland, Ron Ruskin — CEO's and friends.

Let me explain: Traditionally, buyers were responsible for planning their department's sales six months at a time. They would estimate a monthly sales goal, plan the amount of inventory they'd need to achieve that goal, figure in certain factors such as markdowns, and then determine how much money to commit to buying new product. This money (called the "open-to-buy" in industry terminology) would then be allocated by the buyer at her discretion across the various manufacturers she was typically buying from.

The manufacturer never knew how much of a buyer's total open-to-buy they were going to get when she walked into the showroom. As far as the money she had to spend on merchandise – you were lumped in with all your competitors. If she liked the competitors' new collection better than she liked yours, she'd buy more from them and less from you. And that's the way it was, until we changed it.

What we were now asking the retailers and their buyers to do was to commit their dollars months in advance exclusively to Liz Claiborne before even seeing the new line.

This was a major breakthrough. The buyer would no longer have the power to divide up her dollars any way she wanted to. She would be locked in – committed in advance to spending those dollars on our merchandise. In a sense the new process took the decision-making away from the store and the entire market and put it in the hands of one supplier, Liz Claiborne.

The stores were primed to take this step because of the incredible success they were having with our clothing and because that success allowed us to form relationships with the stores' upper management. It wasn't just the assigned buyer who was coming in to see the merchandise, it was merchandise managers, and, in a great number of cases, store presidents as well. We were a phenomenon, we were making exciting things happen in their stores, and so the retail executives were very interested in checking us out. Their visits gave us the opportunity to build strong bonds with them, and it was a job I loved doing.

We presented the department concept to the stores that we were most involved with, which included Saks, Bloomingdale's, the J. L. Hudson Company in Detroit, a number of the Macy's stores, as well as the Dayton Company in Minneapolis, Lazarus in Columbus, Ohio, and many of the Federated stores.

When we approached Saks, the company's executives expressed the natural concern that the buyer would be giving up control and discretionary decision-making over how much of the Liz line to buy since it would have already been blocked out in the plans.

But we had some pluses on our side. Our business with Saks had been growing and we were on our way to becoming one of the largest resources in their retail organization. The Saks buyer who worked with us, Ellen Daniel, had been involved with Liz ever since our company started and had been one of our original boosters.

So in spite of their reservations, Saks decided to go with the concept. We got our department number, and Ellen began to concentrate only on Liz.

With Liz & Kitty Haines of Bamberger's, one of our first dedicated buyers.

I recently spoke with Burt Tansky, who was the general merchandise manager at Saks Fifth Avenue at the time we were campaigning to get our own department number. Burt is an outstanding apparel merchant who got his start in 1961 in the training program at Kaufman's Department Store in Pittsburgh. He has been president and CEO of Neiman Marcus since 2002 and just retired. Burt and I were particularly close during all the years he was with Saks.

I asked Burt how he remembers the process playing out. His reply was music to my ears. "It was probably the best move we ever made," he said. "It created concentration, motivation, and focus on building one particular business in our stores."

For years Liz remained the single largest supplier to Saks, even though we were on the low end of the store's product pricing structure.

Interestingly, Burt told me that he took the Liz Claiborne example and applied it to a few other manufacturers throughout the store and was by and large very pleased with the results.

At any rate, as is typical in the world of retail, when we got the first few stores to agree to a department number, everyone else fell in line. It helped that we had high credibility and were seen as a new and different kind of manufacturer who could be trusted with these responsibilities. Among other things, it was well known that we cared much more about the consumers' response to our merchandise than just getting an order from a store. The stores' managements understood the importance of our attitude and were appreciative.

Another plus in our favor was that our sales force and our managers understood the world that the retailers were operating in and could speak their language. They were at least as skilled as the buyers themselves in understanding retail math, the markdown, gross margin and all of the problems that the store faced. Again, this made us completely different from any other company that these buyers were dealing with.

Getting our own department was a wonderful and dangerous position for us to be in. It put a tremendous amount of power into our hands, but at the same time we were now under a microscope. We had to continue to perform well at the retail level, never lose touch with the consumer and avoid any missteps. Otherwise, our credibility would disappear very quickly.

Once the department concept was established, we would make our sales plans together with the buyers from each participating retailer so that they – and we – knew what their open-to-buy would be.

We'd sit with the buyers and figure it all out. We would get the total dollars figure, and we'd have to break it down by the different categories we were manufacturing. Eventually it would get broken down further to styles and colors for the upcoming line – How many skirts? How many *styles* of skirts? How many colors? And then, of course, each of these factors would have to be broken down by individual branch store. There were enormous volume differences between the top and bottom stores with every retailer.

The process gave us a complete picture of how they were going to do business with Liz Claiborne. They were telling us in advance what we could expect. And we were helping them figure it out. Up until then there was no such thing as this kind of a partnership between a retailer and a manufacturer. Under the partnership, we became an increasingly important resource for the store, and it gave us confidence that we would not suddenly become unimportant and lose business the next season. But we understood there were no guarantees of any kind.

Now we had a handle on the logistical challenges we faced every season in planning, production, and distribution.

Once this process was well under way, we quickly followed up with the department store management and convinced them that the buyer working with us should be a *dedicated* buyer – she should work only for the Liz Claiborne department in the store. We didn't want her to have any other responsibilities with any other manufacturer. My basic pitch was, "We want to build the Liz Claiborne department, and you know we will do enough volume so that her salary can be amortized."

The stores were willing to try it.

The ones that bought into the concept did a far better job than those that didn't. And once the industry saw that the idea was working, other retailers came to us and wanted to join in. It couldn't work at all with the specialty stores because their volume was too small.

But it worked with the biggest retailers and everybody benefited. So here was a case where we broke a rule, did something different, and made it work for ourselves, our customers, and the consumer. It was the ultimate chutzpah to think that we could pull it off, but we did.

Two marketplace factors were very important in helping make these breakthroughs successful with the retailers and with the consumers --

First, we were getting incredible support from the fashion magazines. The Liz consumer was precisely the person these publications were serving. So they would put our merchandise in the editorial pages with stories and articles featuring our latest designs.

The fashion editors would come in to see us at the very beginning of the season and look at the line. We were in such demand that a squabble sometimes took place over which magazines would show which garments. They were all there: *Glamour, Mademoiselle, Vogue,* and *Harper's Bazaar.*

We were getting such tremendous coverage from the editorial sections of these magazines that it actually led to another rule breaker: no national advertising. We didn't need to buy the ads. There was just no point in spending money to advertise in those same magazines that were giving us such good coverage. The rule of thumb in the industry is that editorial is worth at least three to four times as much as an advertisement in the same magazine. So why advertise?

Now it is true that we did have a co-op advertising program. If a store wanted to run a Liz Claiborne ad in their local paper, we would participate. We would also put co-op money into store catalogues, which in those days they used to publish in the spring and in the fall.

But on the national stage, we just wouldn't do it. We were getting the coverage, and that worked just fine. At one point not many years later, *Women's Wear Daily* did a piece on the best known brands in America, and we were at the top – the first or second best known brand in America – and we had never advertised nationally.

Besides having the fashion magazines on our side, the other marketplace factor that helped us enormously was the location of the Liz Claiborne departments inside the department stores. We took a very strong position on this issue. Again, as a former retailer, I understood very well how important store location was and where and how we wanted the consumer to see our product. So as soon as we became an important department, we insisted that the stores give us a prime location. In most department stores, the better apparel departments where the Liz merchandise would be displayed were on the second floor. We wanted our department to be located at the right hand side of the escalator coming up to the second floor as soon as the consumer got off. That way, the first thing she would see going up to the better apparel area would be us.

Our approach to the stores was to convince them it was for their benefit. "Now that we have these departments, we want you to be more successful with our merchandise. And the easier and better you make it for your consumer, the better your sell through and your volume is going to be. So why not take full advantage of the Liz department concept?" It did make sense, and the store managers knew it and usually agreed.

With all of these issues, the fact that we spoke the retailers' language and understood their point of view meant that we could usually overcome objections. We would make it clear that we had their best interests at heart – and in fact we honestly did. They had given us a lot of power with the department number, the dedicated buyer, the prime locations, but we all saw it as a responsibility as well, and we let them know it. We didn't want to take advantage of our new position with the retailers, we wanted to live up to it.

We created a process for merchandising our line that would fulfill our responsibilities to the retailer and to the consumer. Our line and process meetings were held on a regular basis as we prepared each collection. Attending were Liz and any other designers that she felt should be present, Art, and other fabric people. I would be present as a representative, in a sense, of the retailer and the consumer.

Liz would present the ideas that she had for the line, usually first in sketches, and we would talk about them. The sketches would then be turned into samples that we would examine and discuss at a subsequent meeting. In every case we were very, very careful to create a collection that would take full advantage of our retail department situation and would satisfy the needs of the consumer – mainly by making sure all the items would go together. We also very consciously tried to include special items in every collection both to help with the sell through and also to create additional excitement. Most often they were tops. When we started producing sweaters around 1979, we would make a special effort to turn them into exciting articles of clothing that would raise the level of interest in the whole collection. People just loved these kinds of items.

We were very careful in trying to understand how the consumer was actually buying our merchandise and to plan accordingly. We knew for example, how important tops were. We knew customers bought more tops than bottoms. In putting together an outfit, she might buy two blouses and a sweater and only one skirt. In order for the retailer to have the appropriate kind of inventory, we would have to make sure to put the merchandise into work so that it would be on the sales floor in appropriate quantity at the same time and all together. It was always an estimate on our part.

It sounds simple, but it was always a logistical nightmare. As the company grew, we had to increase our manufacturing capability by opening factories in many different countries. The items in our collection had to be color coordinated and arrive back in the States at the same time. This was not a simple job because often a color-matched blouse and skirt were produced in different countries. Our manufacturing people, led by Leonard Boxer, developed a variety of quality control systems to insure that everything came out the way we wanted it to. We weren't perfect, and over the years we had some hair-raising experiences with tops that didn't match bottoms, but by and large, our track record was excellent.

I can't say enough about the importance of the production side of our company, which allowed us to increase our sales geometrically and still deliver the quality product that our consumers demanded. When I left the company, we had 8000 employees, none of whom were involved in the actual sewing of garments. If we were to include all the sewers, cutters, and other workers in all the companies we contracted with to create our product, we would be talking about 100,000 employees spread all over the world. And we had to manage them all!

Jack Listanowsky: The Challenges of Global Production

The design and sales teams kept challenging the production team that I headed to keep up with them. It felt like each season we were expected to produce double the volume of goods. In order to give you an idea of this growth, we were talking about the hundreds of thousands of garments each and every month. As growth continued, it became millions of garments every month. These were staggering numbers.

If it were only simple t-shirts and basic twill pants and jeans we were producing, it would have been tough. But the kinds of garments we were dealing with were incredibly complex: blazers, skirts, blouses of all fabrics and shapes, sweaters and other knit clothing, coordinated in every way they could dream up! This was a real nightmare. And it was compounded by the fact that we weren't just buying the fabrics and yarns in the same country that we were producing the garments. Instead, we were buying fabrics and yarns made in one country and then shipping them to another country for assembly.

Could it get any more complicated? Well, yes it could. We also had to deal with quota limits that the United States placed on the countries producing these goods. The quotas established the number of any particular kind of garment that could be produced in the country and shipped to the US. For instance, Hong Kong was limited to X number of, say, cotton sweaters that it could manufacture for US apparel companies.

There were times when Liz Claiborne's appetite for cotton sweaters alone exceeded all of Hong Kong's allowed quota!

So the only way we could get our hands on all the sweaters – or any other category of garment – we needed was to expand the number of countries where we could have our garments made.

Now we are talking about a couple of million cotton sweaters every 120 days. Then we had to deal with cotton jackets or cotton pants, for which there was also huge demand, and each with its own quota category restrictions.

We had to begin sourcing literally on a global basis. The world became the Liz Claiborne production department's supermarket. Each garment-producing country had to be evaluated for its quota holdings. Factories in each of these countries needed to be vetted for their skills and product capacities. Quality had to be controlled. Timely shipping had to be assured. And all along the companies' product demands escalated. We had to be vigilant at every step of the production process. Our work had changed dramatically since the time I first started working at Liz Claiborne in 1981. It was a wild, risky, exciting ride!

As we thought about consumer behavior on the floor of the store, we recognized that we had another serious problem we had to deal with.

Liz was designing merchandise that allowed a consumer to pick items within a coordinated group with the assurance that they would work together as an outfit. We shipped these groups so that they would be appropriately presented on the floor and so that the customer coming into the department would see them to best advantage. In my own mind, I used to hear the customer say, "Ok, I see lots of skirts, blouses, jackets, and sweaters I can choose from. I can pick what I like, and I don't have to worry about what goes with what. I know that any of the pieces I buy will work together because Liz tells me so. I don't have to think about it."

It's almost as if she could buy blindfolded. But it was vitally important that all the items be kept together the way we intended. We were moving heaven and earth to deliver them, and they might start being displayed together, but in the course of the shopping day, it's practically guaranteed that everything will get mixed up. What happens when items are taken to the fitting room and left there or are returned to the wrong rack?

We also typically had several different groups on the floor at the same time so that mixing up the merchandise could confuse the consumer and the salesperson (if there was one) and affect sales.

Here again, it's important to understand that our organization was filled with former retailers who knew what the day-to-day problems were at the retail level. Who in the world would think that we had to worry about where the merchandise is placed when it's brought back from the ladies fitting room?

Well, we did. And we wrestled with the problem.

We decided that the way to solve it was to give each of our groups a *name* and *put the name on the ticket*. Believe it or not, this was a revolutionary idea at the time.

A group might be given a name like *Fall Reflections,* and all of the pieces – sweaters, blouses, skirts, pants, jackets, and so on – would have a ticket on them with the group name. From now on, consumers would know that if the ticket says *Fall Reflections,* it goes with all of the other items of the same name.

Sales people could now be told that when they bring clothes back from the fitting room, or as they are tidying up the sales floor, they must look for the name on the ticket and make sure the item of clothing is returned to its proper area.

It was a small thing, and looking back, it was an obvious thing to do. But it was revolutionary when we did it. Within six months, all of our competitors followed suit and were naming their groups. But we did it first!

All the innovations large and small would add up to a vast change in the way retailers looked at their business. The department stores of America were set up in a particular way when we started Liz Claiborne. They had their specific classifications and their manufacturers for each one of them.

Here we came along with a company making clothing for all of the different classifications of merchandise. Once they found a place for us and the Liz Claiborne areas started to grow and prosper across the country, it didn't take very long for some of our competitors to decide that if there was business being done in coordinated separates, then maybe they should be in that business.

The competition grew and multiplied over the years. Companies like Evan Picone, Leslie Fay, and Jones New York, which made clothing spread over many different classifications – skirts, jackets, blouses, pants, etc. – began to pull together their separates into coordinated groupings that could be presented to the consumer in a boutique-like setting mimicking the Liz Claiborne departments. They were going after some of those Liz Claiborne open to buy dollars from the department stores.

As we broke the classification rules, and as others followed, department stores were forced to take a good look at how they were setting up their apparel areas. All of a sudden it became apparent to them that instead of going by classification as they had been for years, they were better off setting it up by manufacturer. So that there would be a Liz Claiborne area, an Evan Picone area, a Jones New York area, a Leslie Fay area, etc. Remarkably, the shift to the label set up took no more than a year, or a perhaps year and a half after we started it.

Department stores are still set up this way. It's ironic, but I occasionally hear from women friends who get very upset about this. They go to a department store to buy, say, a pair of black pants, and they are forced to march all around the store to all the different name-brand departments to see what's available. "Why," they'll ask me, "Can't all the black pants be together so I can shop in one spot and find what I want? " Well, I guess that's my fault – Liz Claiborne's fault. I wish I could say I'm sorry, but I wouldn't have it any other way.

Men's departments have not been immune from all these changes. I think a lot of men get confused and unhappy in today's department store. If they are shopping for a simple blue blazer, they want all of them to be in one place where they can look at a few, try on a couple, and get on with it. They don't want to go through all the different designers' areas looking and shopping, trying to figure out which designer works best for them. I know that I sometimes experience the same frustration when I am shopping for myself.

All in all, I think men pay less attention to the label and more attention to their specific, immediate needs – a blazer is a blazer is a blazer. Women, thank goodness, seem to care so much about the label that if they can't find exactly what they want from the designer they're currently in love with, they won't buy anything. They'll come back at another time to look for the item. It was certainly that way at the beginning of Liz and as the company grew. People walked in to the Liz department and acted like they didn't know that there was any other merchandise in the store. This was where they wanted to be; this was the kind of merchandise they wanted to see; this was where they were happy buying. Even if they couldn't find exactly what they came in to buy, they were sure that there was something in the department that would work for them.

Lee & Marvin Traub – At a book signing.

So here we are. Our innovations led to the look of today's department store, where merchandise is shown boutique by boutique, designer by designer. Will the system ever change? Will we ever get back to some sort of mixture between classification and the so-called boutique approach? I guess it remains to be seen. Right now we're in the age of boutiques, and I think we'll remain there for a while.

I do think that the huge success we had with our Liz departments may have inspired some people in the business to start thinking that they could create a Liz Claiborne kind of specialty operation for their own brands and operate in a similar fashion for their consumers. A case could be made that the inspiration and the example we provided, plus one other factor – the proliferation of regional malls all across the country – helped spark drastic changes in the nature of specialty stores, forcing them to evolve from mom-and-pop type operations to the huge chains like the Gap, the Limited, and Abercrombie & Fitch, who now dominate the specialty store landscape.

In the old days, before the regional malls were built, small privately owned and operated specialty stores were a significant part of the apparel industry. They supplemented the department stores by scouring the apparel market for special merchandise not easily available elsewhere and offering the consumer more personalized treatment. It was very much the world of Winkelman's that I had spent such valuable time in, but unlike Winkelman's, which was one of the few specialty stores to grow into a large chain, they were usually small, family run stores with just a couple of locations. There were thousands of them around the country selling the products of a multitude of small apparel manufacturers.

The rise of the regional mall put evolutionary forces into play that foreshadowed the demise of many of these specialty stores. As the malls were being built with astonishing speed across the country, developers began to look for well-financed retailers to occupy them. Aside from the department stores that traditionally "anchor" the mall at each end, the mall operators began to look for deep pocket tenants to fill the rest of the space in between. The need was driven by the banks, which had lent enormous sums of money to the developers and wanted assurances that the mall tenants could pay their rents to the mall operator in good times and bad, so that in turn the operator could meet his obligations to the banks. Unfortunately, many of the mom-and-pop operations had little cash and limited lines of credit. They just didn't fit into this new business model. Instead, a new group of well-financed, prosperous companies began to emerge and establish themselves as the preferred tenants for the malls.

One of the leaders in this new movement was the Limited stores which started in Ohio and spread like wildfire around the country. The Limited was soon joined by other new-specialty retailers like Casual Corner and

Talbots. These stores shopped the apparel market, bought from a variety of manufacturers and presented the merchandise to the consumer.

Wall Street loved and encouraged this new business model of retailing. As investors, they saw it as a very simple cookie cutter play. They would find stores to invest in while they were still relatively small and then help replicate the store many times over in as many new malls as possible.

Many of these new specialty stores took a page or two from the Liz playbook: design the goods in America and produce them offshore. The Limited, for one, seemed to have learned a lot from us. We recognized what these new specialty stores were doing but couldn't help also noticing that no matter what they did, they couldn't copy our creativity. Instead, they would appropriate important looks that were in the market and identify current "hot" styles to copy for future seasons. Most of the merchandise they sold was very basic, with a heavy emphasis on pants, skirts, and sweaters. In spite of the nature of the product, the new breed of specialty store flourished as consumers enjoyed the convenience of driving out to the mall.

So specialty store vertical retailing was born, gestated, and today it completely dominates the apparel industry. Virtually every specialty store you can name has become a vertical retailer: Abercrombie & Fitch, the Gap, J. Crew, Eddie Bauer, Ann Taylor, Talbots, and dozens of others. Some of them have even managed to put together their own excellent creative departments, and so in a way have become copies of what a manufacturer used to do, but for only one customer: their own stores. Mickey Drexler, once at Anne Taylor, then at the Gap, and now at J. Crew, saw this new way of doing business and was especially adept at making it work.

You could make the case that it all started with Liz. And, truth be told, many of the most successful of the vertical retailers were originally Liz buyers or merchandise managers. They got their training with us, absorbed our concepts, and then they went out and did it themselves.

The growth of these specialty stores in many ways paralleled the growth of Liz, since much of our expansion came about as department stores were anchoring all these new malls. As more and more branch locations popped up in the malls, they needed vastly more amounts of inventory, and Liz Claiborne supplied it. Throughout this expansion period, the Liz departments remained tremendously successful in these stores.

But the way in which most department stores were doing business during this period of rapid growth was becoming a concern to us. We had lived through a major proliferation of branch stores, especially in the 1980s. In many cases, the stores had bitten off more than they could chew and expanded too quickly. Many of the branch stores simply weren't doing enough volume to justify the expense of running them. At some point, the industry realized their problem and suddenly turned to cost-cutting as a remedy. It became a craze of sorts. Unfortunately many of the cuts took place in the sales organizations among the personnel who interacted with the customers and sold the merchandise to them. I would think that would be the last place to make cuts, but cut they did. And the more they cut, the more their volume suffered.

The cutbacks drastically affected coverage on the floor. It became impossible to find a sales person. What took place then is still very true today: if a customer wanted an item, she would have to hunt for a salesperson to help her. She would even have to hunt for a salesperson to pay for her purchase after finding the correct rack on her own, picking out the item by herself, and finding the fitting room by herself. Now all she wanted to do was pay for it, and she couldn't even find someone to give the money to!

On top of this, some of the earliest cuts were made in personnel once considered essential to the stores, such as the display people who changed the mannequins and kept the departments in tiptop shape for the customer. Some retailers got rid of so many of these people in the branches that the face of the store and the face of the merchandise that the consumer saw went from bad to worse.

This unfortunate situation led to another innovation –

We were forced to step in and establish our own servicing organization. We began sending people into the department stores to straighten out the Liz Claiborne areas and make sure that our displays and our merchandise looked the way they should.

We then went ahead and took on another role that some might argue should have been the retailers'—

What should have been happening in the stores is that the buyer would visit the branches and educate the salespeople about the merchandise. But it wasn't happening. Buyers were purchasing for so many branches that they didn't have a chance to visit them let alone take the opportunity to talk about the merchandise with the salespeople.

We did the best we could to fill the information gap for the salespeople. We began sending out literature to the individual branch stores about our current collections – about fabric, design, care information, etc., in the hope that the managers would pass it along to the salespeople, the few that were left anyway, who in turn could be helpful to the customers.

The poor condition of the department stores was also reflected in the fact that most of them were not fixtured properly to display Liz Claiborne merchandise to its best advantage. In order to deal with that situation, we came up with our Liz Claiborne shop concept. The idea was to put our merchandise on the right kinds of fixtures with the right kind of hangers – all in an effort to make it more attractive to the consumer.

When the program started we thought the store should pay for these fixtures. Some did. Very quickly however, it turned into a partnership deal where we paid for part of the fixturing and the store paid for part.

Eventually it turned into: "If you want new fixtures in our store, pay for them yourself."

Chapter 5

Creating a Nation of Lizzies

I think I've gotten a little bit ahead of our story. Right now I'd like to go back and deal with a more chronological approach to the growth and expansion of our company.

The success of our early years was stunning, even staggering. Of course we wanted to continue our rapid pace of growth, but we wanted to control it, and so we began to look for prudent and smart ways to expand.

In deciding what we should do next, it became apparent to us that we "owned" a particular consumer. Our early success had created what we liked to think of as a "nation of Lizzies." We believed that the future of the company was with these consumers, and we developed an almost maniacal focus on her and her needs. We made it part of our corporate DNA. And while it might be more obvious today than it was 30 years ago, this focus was vastly different from that of other apparel manufacturers, who seemed more interested in pleasing the department store buyers and their bosses. Our relentless focus on the consumer was something different in the industry. We knew that ultimately our success depended upon *her* purchasing a garment and not just upon a buyer placing the order with us. We made it our job to design products our Lizzies would find appealing and to market them in a way that provided an enjoyable and satisfying shopping experience.

We took this mission so seriously that we made sure new employees, and there were many of them as we were expanding at an astounding pace, understood it and made it part of their working lives. Many of the new hires – salespeople and other employees – had been successful with other apparel companies. But we had to teach them that Liz was a different kind of place, so we worked hard to "Lizify" them, redirecting and refocusing their knowledge to fit the mission and goals of our company.

We thought about our consumer day in and day out. We used to talk about her in the showroom and would try to describe her: what she looked like, where she worked, what kind of job she performed, what kind of family life she enjoyed, how much money she earned, and of course, what her clothing needs and preferences were.

It became obvious to us that growth would come from owning this consumer and addressing *all* her apparel needs, and, as we will see later on, taking care of her accessory needs as well, and even extending into her home with domestic goods, much as the European designer companies were doing.

But I'm getting ahead of myself again –

Our first obvious growth opportunity came to us quickly. We began hearing from some customers and from the stores themselves that there was someone out there who we weren't taking care of – the petite woman. She was 5'2" or smaller, represented as much as 30% of the market, and she was having a very difficult time buying clothes that fit her properly and getting a good selection. There were some other manufacturers already making clothes in petite sizes, but up until now it was handled as a small, niche business. On a personal level, I could see the sense of getting into this market. I was the head of a petite family. My wife and two daughters were all potential customers for a petite line, as they were no more that 5"1' or 5'2' – with a little stretching. So, perhaps I was a little less objective in looking at this potential business than I would have been otherwise.

It almost seemed like this smaller lady was asking us, "Why can't there be a Liz Claiborne for petites?"

And so we answered, "Why not?"

Jan Sommers: Petites at Liz Claiborne

As time went on I was promoted to head up the fledgling Petites Division. Jerry Chazen thought I would be particularly aware of this customer as I was petite too. "But I'm not petite," I told him.

"Oh yes you are!" he replied. "Our job is bigger than I thought if the customer doesn't even know who she is!"

Saks Fifth Avenue had encouraged Jerry to enter this arena, and he appointed me to lead the way for petite women seeking fashion. This line would need to be built from inception. We worked closely with the stores in developing this new market. Who was this petite woman? How did we reach her?

The premise was the same. The line must be presented together as a compelling collection for easy outfit building. No hanging pants and tops and jackets separately. And the racks and shelves must be in easy reach for shorter women. A question came up: Should the items be sized S-M-L, or would the petite customer never relate to a size L - Large? We decided on P-S-M instead. We suggested a petites department be formed in the stores along with other vendors merchandise to become a destination for this consumer.

The job was challenging. Some of Liz's prints were so big that a full repeat of a plaid wouldn't make it onto a size 2 shirt, and so we needed to work with the designers to reduce the patterns. Our fit was at first not petite enough. We had encouraged the stores to buy petite fixtures. And at first our pants on the petite racks were dragging on the floor!

Long skirts did not sell as well as short skirts, and the balance between tops and bottoms was very different in the petite department. Petite women felt pants and skirts were her biggest fit problem — not tops. That meant that I needed to plan the line closer to 1 or 2 tops per bottom, not the traditional 3 or 4 tops per bottom as in most Liz collections.

But we were still Liz Claiborne, and the Petites Division grew to $100 million in sales in two years time!

As carefully and scientifically as possible, Liz and Leonard went through our entire line and came up with an appropriate fit for each garment we were making: blouses, sweaters, pants or jackets. We tailored them specifically for the petite woman in the Liz styles that were appropriate for this woman.

We approached the stores and suggested that they put these petite clothes into a separate area in the store, buy petite merchandise from other manufacturers and create a petites department. That just seemed like good business, plus it would keep the garments from getting mixed in with the Misses apparel – a concern since they looked alike –causing confusion when consumers looked for their sizes. The stores went along for the most part, and the petite Liz became a stronghold in the petite departments in most of the major department stores around the country.

Up until now, virtually all of the Liz merchandise was designed to take care of our Lizzies' more serious daytime needs, whether she was going to the office, or a community meeting, or a luncheon. We felt that we should also start offering her clothing for the more casual moments of her life

We had one big fashion advantage that helped us here. Liz believed in the prevalence of "the pear-shaped woman." She felt that the contour of a pear represented the typical woman's silhouette, and if the garment was made correctly for this woman, it would fit properly and comfortably. This was particularly important for pants, and as Liz herself wore pants and never skirts or dresses, she felt strongly about it. She had developed a pant fit for this woman early on in the company even though her previous design expertise had been in dresses. Women loved it and the pant remained a standard in the company.

Here again, based on both conversation and observation, it was apparent that the most basic need in casual sportswear was a pant. Liz felt it should be cotton and washable. We settled on a twill fabric that met the specs, gave it the great Liz fit, and we had a winner.

Of course you can't have a casual line with just a pant, so we took our "collection" technique and developed the same kind of coordinated looks for casual wear. Consumers loved it and showed their appreciation at the cash register.

So these new casual groups joined the already large stock of wear-to-work clothes. You might have thought we invented a new form of clothing by the way our "Lizzies" were grabbing these garments. As soon as we recognized that we had hit yet another mother lode, we expanded the collection. We also realized that it was all plus business since we were addressing her clothing needs for a different part of her life. To avoid confusion with our more serious line, in 1982 we changed the label to Liz Sport and established a new division to handle it.

It's not too difficult to imagine our next move: as the volume of the casual business increased, we asked the stores to create a separate department for this merchandise on their casual floor. It was a little easier convincing them this time around, and so they gave us an additional department number, and in many cases, an additional buyer dedicated only to Liz Sport.

The more casual clothes in the collection, like t-shirts, shorts, and cotton sweaters were less expensive than our more serious Liz Claiborne clothes, and we were able to increase the number of units we were manufacturing dramatically. These clothes also provided a perfect place for us to use our newly designed logo. Our triangle looked great over the pocket of a shirt or on the back of a pant or on any other place we could tastefully get this identification across. Over the next few years, along with the growth of the company, our logo became as important as the Ralph Lauren polo player.

Everything worked well with Liz Sport, and the new label made a major contribution to the growth of our company.

Now, with more than one department number at many of our customers, our planning process with the stores became more complicated and even more significant. Our volume levels had already passed some of the highest numbers that these stores had ever seen. Now we had to ask, "How high is up?" We wanted to challenge ourselves to grow our volume, but we didn't want to get carried away, as uncontrolled growth can lead to big problems down the road, including gluts of inventory that I certainly witnessed in my days as a retailer.

We knew that in order to be accurate, our planning had to be done "bottom-up," encompassing each of the branch stores in each of the chains we were selling to. We knew how all of our customers were doing, so we could use the best performances of certain stores and apply them to other ones. That way the branch would be properly supplied.

We gathered as much information as we could from our retail customers regarding our own performance in their stores and found that two very useful measures were first, the percentage of the women's apparel business in each branch and, second, the percentage of total store sales we were responsible for. It was harder to get information on the first measure because even though we had a fabulous relationship with the department stores, many were loath to give us specific information about competitor sales. So we found it easier to measure our sales performance in each door (as each branch was called) as a percentage of the store's total sales volume.

We also used our knowledge of our customers' business to boost sales in stores that we thought had not yet reached full potential. We would use the total volume figures as an indication of how many people were coming into the branch. Then we would go through our customer list and find out which stores with similar volumes were doing the best job selling our merchandise From there we could show the laggard stores what stores just like their own were doing – stores with similar volume and demographics. This would give them a boost when they would see what was possible and realistic in terms of increasing sales of Liz Claiborne. The logic we could show them behind our projections would give them comfort and assure them that we weren't indulging in pie-in-the-sky planning. We would then be able to convince them that they could be more successful if they did the right planning, allocated the right amount of space, and purchased the right amount of merchandise from us. Obviously, as the volume plans increased, stores had to give additional space to Liz Claiborne, and so we would become more and more dominant on the sales floor.

All of the information we were gathering from our customers brought us to an interesting conclusion: we could become 1% of a store's total volume. We made it a goal. We should aim for having our merchandise be responsible for 1% of a store's total business!

Now the Liz Claiborne sales force had goals to work towards that we could all measure. And it set up exciting challenges as the individual sales people sought to reach these goals. We also found that the retailers liked the concept and began setting up contests in their branches to do more Liz Claiborne business and attempt to reach the 1% goals themselves. What could be nicer than having our own customers, the retailers, stretching to sell more of our merchandise? It was just another way of doing business that made Liz different from all of the other manufacturers.

As we broke through historical volume levels at many stores, contributing far more sales than any one apparel company normally did, management from the store president on down began to look at their own volume potential differently. It was a kind of epiphany for them – and they began looking at ways of doing more business rather than holding Liz sales (and others as well) down to a preplanned number.

A number of studies at the time had shown that a typical department store did business with thousands of different suppliers with no real effort being made to concentrate on any of them. It's quite possible that the Liz experience helped to change retail thinking and influenced them to focus on fewer suppliers.

As we talked to stores about the amount of business we were doing and could potentially do, management would often bring up the name Estee Lauder, one of the most important cosmetic and fragrance companies in the world. As our own volume grew, Estee Lauder became our challenge – the one we had to beat – in terms of volume and importance to the stores. We were in a completely different business, of course, and not competitive. But unknown to Leonard Lauder (until he reads this), his company did become our rival in the chase to be the number one department store supplier.

Our company was growing, and we were working happily and harmoniously with the retailers in a way that is almost impossible to fathom today. Nowadays, the business isn't so much fun, with retailers and manufacturers fighting over pennies. The industry had not yet become markdown or sale crazy. Stores thought about quality and they appealed to the customer by offering the right fashion rather than the cheapest price. It's so different today that it almost seems like we must have been living in a fairyland back then.

I recently spoke with David Farrell, the retired CEO of the May Company about today's retail scene. He agreed with my own point of view. He said, "It's a tough world out there. Unfortunately in today's environment, it's very difficult to make the kind of returns that Liz Claiborne and the May Company used to make. There are a few companies out there like Wal-Mart, Costco who are doing it, but for the most part, the business just doesn't give shareholders a hell of a lot of return for their investment."

We talked about other consumer-oriented industries that seem able to do a big business at the retail level. David mentioned Apple and the fact that it is doing close to $7 billion in their own stores. He was kind enough to add, "Apple is in many ways the Liz Claiborne of today. They do wonderful design!"

I was curious to know how he felt about Liz Claiborne's rapid growth and the way in which we came to dominate the market. I asked, "Were you ever concerned that the company was getting too big even for big retailers like May Company? Did you ever think you were doing too much business with us? Did that bother you?"

His answer left no doubt that he never had a concern but instead welcomed our growth, "No. Liz Claiborne had a wonderful business system and the more places that you applied it to, the better off we were."

In fact, our growth was so fast, everything was going so well, and our future looked so good that, in spite of the youth of our company, we decided that we should offer shares in the company to investors. The year was 1980 and Liz Claiborne decided to go public.

This decision to go public evolved as we found ourselves already being courted by companies that wanted to buy us. One of the biggest public apparel companies at the time was Hart Schaffner Marx in Chicago, a men's clothing company with virtually no exposure at all to the women's market. They sent some representatives to visit us and suggested a merger. They had absolutely no interest in changing anything that we were doing; instead, we would be a completely autonomous unit and continue to run our company the way we wanted to run it. One of the benefits of the deal was that Hart could provide capital if we needed capital, although we were turning our inventory so frequently we didn't need it. We weren't borrowing any money either. But it would be available if needed. Another plus was that it would be an opportunity for the four partners to cash out a little bit – to sell some small percentages of our ownership, which was now worth a lot more than our initial investments in the company.

We were pleased that a company like Hart had sought us out, but as we looked into their company, we realized that a merger could prevent us from running our business our way. They were having big problems with the men's clothing workers unions and were being forced to continue to do all of their manufacturing in the US, even though some of their competitors were going overseas and offering comparable quality merchandise at much lower prices. In the end, we really didn't see the advantage of tying up with that kind of a company, so we reluctantly said, "Thanks, but no thanks."

There were some other efforts to buy us. Carl Rosen, for one, who was the CEO of Puritan Sportswear and a legend in the industry, signaled that we would be a nice company to add to his collection.

This kind of activity got us thinking about the future, the growing value of our ownership stakes and about how we could safeguard the company against major financial disasters. For example: what would happen if one of the founding partners should die – how could we pay the partner's estate for his or her ownership portion as required by law, without crippling the company?

Because of my financial background, I knew that there were some real benefits to going public. We could make sure that the principals of Liz Claiborne and their heirs were taken care of if something terrible should happen to any of them, and at the same time we would be able to continue to grow the company. Also not to be sneezed at was the fact that by going public each of us would get a nice financial reward for our success so far. For the first time in our lives we would have some serious capital of our own.

We discussed these issues with our advisory board and our attorneys. They felt that even though we were still a relatively young company, not quite five years in business, the maturity and experience of the four founders, the success that we had been having and the story that we had to tell would generate interest on Wall Street.

We approached the investment bankers, including Bear Stearns, Goldman Sachs, and Morgan Stanley. These large firms had all participated in a wave of apparel companies going public in the 1960s. Unfortunately, virtually all of those companies went bankrupt, famous name companies like Jonathan Logan, Leslie Fay, and Villager. This first group of bankers we spoke with still didn't trust the apparel industry, and so while they listened, they didn't believe that the fashion industry was worthy of investment.

One company we met with saw things differently, and that was Merrill Lynch. The Merrill Lynch banker we met with was much younger than other Wall Street people we had seen up to that point. His name was Ray Minella, and Ray bought our story. He listened to us and liked the idea. He understood our consumer. He didn't have any built-in bias about the industry and, like us, saw the potential for growth at Liz Claiborne. At one of our meetings, he brought the Merrill apparel analyst with him, a lady by the name of Brenda Gall. She was more familiar with our product and our industry than Ray was, and to make a long story short, they decided to take us on and help us go public. Brenda, by the way, went on to a long and distinguished career and followed our company until the day she retired.

After signing up with Merrill, we began the process of stoking interest in our stock within the investment community through "road shows," (we thought of them as dog and pony shows) where we would meet with institutional investors, tell them our story and try to get them interested in buying our stock. I became the face of the company for this process.

It was the spring of 1981, and we were riding high. Our original investors, the ones who had faith in us from the beginning and put up money to help us start the company, had been patiently waiting for something like this to happen and were perhaps even more anxious than the four partners for the public offering to take place. For some of these initial investors, it was cash out time.

For me, it was the Wall Street game itself that was most enthralling. I had read about other companies going public, but being engaged in the process, having *our* company participate was an exciting and fascinating experience. It was almost as if there was a "chase" mentality in trying to come up with an appropriate valuation for the Company and, of course, a stock price that matched it. In the five years since we had started the company, our volume had grown to $79 million. Based upon the first quarter results of 1981, it looked as if we would have a very substantial increase for the year. In fact, by years' end, our volume had increased to almost $117 million.

It was a very heady time, but like many things in life, sadness entered the picture. Right in the middle of the road show travels, my mother became very ill, went into the hospital, and within a few days, passed away. It was a tough situation to deal with. I remember that Ray Minella, in particular, was extremely solicitous, and it turned out that his mom was a grief counselor, and he offered her services. It was just an indication of what a nice guy he was.

I knew my mother would have been so proud. She loved Liz and particularly respected her design talent. It is very ironic, but it turned out that my mother had been a dress designer herself in the early part of the twentieth century. She even had an opportunity to go into business with a partner, but she turned down the offer. She quit her job when she got married in 1919 and that was the end of her career. She never talked about that period of her life, and she only told me about her early work in the garment industry when she was elderly – and long after I had embraced my own opportunity to start Liz Claiborne.

Merrill Lynch, in its ultimate wisdom, came up with a valuation for the company which would have set a price on the stock from $13 to $15 a share. As we told our story on the road and as Merrill got information back from their representatives in the field, things started to look up for us. One dynamic factor in our favor was the beginning of the "explosion" of women entering the workforce and Wall Street analysts figuring out which companies would most benefit from this major sociological change. Since Liz was almost exclusively dedicated to this new and powerful consumer, we could be considered a "pure play." This approach resonated very strongly at the road shows, and it soon became apparent that our opening share price should be raised. I very much enjoyed what was happening and had a difficult time understanding why Merrill didn't feel even stronger about the potential of the Company.

In determining the market value of Liz Claiborne, a dollar amount that would get translated into the price of an individual share of our stock, the investment banker and Liz had to perform a balancing act. We wanted as high a price as possible for the piece of the company we were selling, but at the same time, we needed a price that investors would find attractive.

At any rate, as is typical in many initial public offerings, Merrill adjusted the price range to $16 - $19 per share. I wanted a $20 share price. It was a nice round number and I felt we deserved that valuation. Then Ray introduced me to Marty Kaplan, one of Merrill's top brokers, and he made me conscious of a Wall Street reality. Merrill, and Marty in particular, who represented top institutional clients, had their own limit. His message: "Above $19 – I walk." Marty represented a lot of buying power and he was telling us that he wouldn't offer our stock to his clients if the price went over $19. This would have been a disaster, so we settled. The issue sold out at that $19 and we never looked back. Over the following ten years, the performance of the stock made us the best IPO in the history of Merrill Lynch.

I saw Ray recently. He had just announced his retirement as a vice chairman of Jeffries & Company. We talked about the IPO and thirty years melted away for both of us as we relived those times. His memory was better than mine. He hasn't forgotten the excitement of those days, and he reminded me of a funny poem he had written about the experience. He based it on Edgar Allan Poe's "The Raven," and it is about my stubborn insistence that Merrill raise the offering price. Here are a couple of sample stanzas:

As I scribbled, tired and weary
Over prospectus proofs so dreary,
Pondering some arcane section
Only lawyers read,
As I scribbled, almost dozin'
Came a bluster and a bludgeon
Thump in, at my office door.

With a chubby hand he gestured
At the document we'd reg'stered
At the place that lawyers go
To sleep and dream.
With a grimace, not with grinnin'
And with eyes bright coals (not twinklin')
He pointed at the price range mentioned
As on cover page of yore
Quoth the Chazen, "Even more!"

We ended up raising about $6,000,000 for the company. In addition, each of the four founders of Liz Claiborne received a check from Merrill for over $2,000,000 – a wonderful payday by any measure but an extraordinary one when you realize that we had each invested only $25,000 initially. We were being rewarded for all of our hard work – our "sweat equity" – and our smart decisions. The money came to us because we were in effect selling a piece of our ownership stake in the business.

It was a big moment for all of us, and it was the first seven-figure check I had ever received. I was so proud of that check. I showed it to my wife and the rest of my immediate family and wished that my parents had still been alive to see it.

Before the public offering, each of had owned 16.71 percent of the company. Now, each owned a reduced amount: 11.18 percent. Together, we no longer had a majority interest in Liz Claiborne. Our private investors also did very well, reaping sums many, many times over their initial investments.

The "market cap" of Liz Claiborne, Inc., stood at $66,111,000 on the day we went public. That figure represented the company's total shares (3.4 million) multiplied by the share price ($19 on the day of the offering). In effect, the stock market was telling the world that we had taken our initial capital investment of $250,000 and had turned it into $66 million in just five years!

Now that we were a "public" company with shareholders all around the country if not the world, a huge sense of responsibility settled on me. Whereas before I was driven to make the company bigger, better, and still more successful, now I became bound and determined to increase the value of the company and the stock and do everything that I could to make the financial community proud of Liz Claiborne. Looking ahead another ten years to the end of 1991, Liz Claiborne stock stood at $42 a share, which was a market cap of $3.589 billion – that's fifty times what it was on the day of our public offering.

I very much relished working with and talking to the analysts, appearing on investment panels, and making sure that Liz Claiborne was getting its just recognition as an excellent, well run public company, and a good investment. I was probably doing the job that typically would be performed by the CFO, but since I understood the financial side and enjoyed doing the work, I just put myself out there and stayed involved.

In a way, maybe I was trying to prove something to myself and to the world. When I left my job at Sutro Brothers and Wall Street early in my career and moved to the Midwest to enter the fashion industry, it could have been seen as a step down in terms of prestige and money. In fact, people thought I was crazy. Or perhaps I just thought of it that way. So here I was all these years later, showing the Street what I could do. Now I was a founder of a great public company, something valued by the Street, and I was showing them and the world that the fashion industry s was an important and exciting place to be. I wanted our company to do a good job for all of our stakeholders, and I have to say we succeeded. We became a growth company with a stock to match and embarked on a decade of record-smashing growth. It was a wonderful, phenomenal time for everybody involved in Liz Claiborne. We made a lot of money for everybody, and the stock price soared.

By the end of the decade following our public offering, we dominated our markets. There's no other way to put it, and I'll devote most of the rest of the book to discussing how we navigated through those years, the many ways in which we expanded, the opportunities and the challenges we faced.

Chapter 6

Conquering New Markets

We found many ways to continue our growth. One of our first moves was to start a ladies dress division. It was a counterintuitive decision. Dress business had been going downhill for many years. When we started our company, in fact, we had thrived on the trend, offering consumers a choice of non-dress clothing. Our success in coordinated sportswear had much to do with the dress decline. Some older consumers never gave up on dresses, but younger people just stopped buying. Most department stores cut back their dress space as they expanded sportswear. As a matter of fact, some smaller branches eliminated their dress departments entirely. Our thinking was that the decline had probably hit bottom, so it might be time for us to step in. Perhaps we could make the kind of dresses that women would like to start wearing again on occasions when they didn't want to wear separates.

We started the dress division in 1982. We brought in a young lady by the name of Harriet Mosson to be in charge. She had been the Liz Claiborne buyer at Macy's when we started the company, and Liz, herself, appreciated Harriet's sense of style and knowledge of manufacturing. She had been very important in the private label ventures at Macy's, so she did have some experience in manufacturing. She had also spent some years as a dress buyer and knew that customer well.

Of course, Liz's own background as a dress designer was very important to the success of the division. While we had hired a separate design team for dresses, Liz had the overall responsibility of deciding which of the styles should be put into production.

Here again, we did things differently from other dress companies, almost all of which were small and operated domestically. We felt that with our production expertise and lower-cost facilities overseas we could offer the consumer better values as well as better designs.

Our entry into the dress business was different and again a rule breaker and we had to work hard to convince department stores to buy into it, but our name certainly helped, as did the look of the line.

Because we were manufacturing our dresses overseas, we were faced with the same timing difficulties that existed in sportswear. Stores would select from our already projected styles. Talk about breaking the rules. This violated everything that had always been sacrosanct about running a successful dress business. The common theme ran something like this: manufacturers would present a large line of samples to choose from. Stores would place small orders for the styles they liked and the manufacturers would then order fabric and eventually deliver. The theory was that the consumer would decide which dresses she liked best and stores could then reorder those styles. Because everything was done domestically and fabrics could be quickly available, these reorders would be delivered in season and so ensure that stocks always reflected what consumers wanted.

But here we were, planning to ship the whole season's total needs up front. There would be no reorders. Stores were aghast. Fortunately, we had our sportswear success behind us and that helped. We had also done our own research on what the most current practices were in the dress area. The fantasy about buy small and then reorder was no longer working. Because of the proliferation of malls and the much larger needs of stores, the old model was ineffective and out of date. Stores were finding themselves with a hodgepodge of styles and leftovers. The only styles that could be reordered were the ones that no one wanted. Actually, planning the seasonal needs up front and selecting the best merchandise they could improved their results. One by one, stores came on board and bought our concept. Within three years our volume hit $87 million. In 1987 it was $141 million, and we proudly announced in our annual report that the division was the largest better dress company in America. We reached our peak volume of $180 million in 1991.

I don't want to give the impression that we were infallible in our business decisions. Not everything we did turned out to be a big success. Here's a prime example:

The year we started the dress division, 1982, was also the year we were approached by one of our major department store customers about starting a girls division that would offer clothing for 7 to 14 year-olds. The store was having a difficult time finding merchandise for this young lady.

They thought – and we thought – that if we selectively applied the Liz Claiborne coordinated line concept to clothing for this younger consumer, we could build a substantial business. The idea seemed so logical that all of us, including some of the retailers we spoke to, thought it would be a big success. We brought in a former children's wear buyer to help us with the new division.

The stores were cautious, but we got orders, albeit small ones. We shipped merchandise in the fall of 1983. Reception was good, and we continued to produce new lines in 1984 and 1985. However we felt like we were struggling and not getting anything close to the consumer acceptance we had gotten in Misses sportswear.

In hindsight, we didn't do enough due diligence. The children's apparel business had become highly promotional and relatively low priced. Quality, it turned out, was not an important factor in these clothes, since kids grow out of them so quickly. Our pricing had ended up being close to our women's sportswear lines. The only saving we could find was in the amount of fabric we were using, since labor costs were the same whether the garment was small or large. So we struggled to price the goods to be competitive and to still make a profit.

In a way, what this market wanted was quite different from what we had been providing the women's clothing market so successfully. Perhaps our higher quality product should have been sold in specialty stores at a higher price, but we had not anticipated nor were we interested in being a small boutique manufacturer. We knew how to sell in large quantity to department stores, so that's where we concentrated our efforts.

Eventually the headaches with price, manufacturing issues, and the general nature of the children's apparel business – we weren't even in a position to dictate how stores presented our merchandise – got to be too great for us. So despite our initial interest in this market, we decided to close it down.

In 1982 our volume had grown to almost $166 million, already making us one of the largest fashion apparel companies in the country. But we continued to talk about growth, and frankly, as we examined the distribution of the company, our outlets, and the growth of our consumer population, we found it impossible to put a ceiling on how much we could grow.

We never lost sight of the fact that we "owned" a consumer. She loved our clothing, loved Liz, and seemed ready to have us take care of all of her clothing needs. As we spoke to retailers and consumers and held discussions in the showrooms and in our partner meetings, we realized that we could add other elements to the clothing that we were manufacturing – there were many other products where a Liz Claiborne label would make sense.

Once a fashion company has developed a recognized brand name, firms in ancillary businesses that think they could make use of the name to sell their own products get into line. They all want to latch on to the latest brand phenomenon. In the case of Liz Claiborne, we entered our first licensing agreement about a year after we went into business, and while we couldn't quite figure out why anyone would want to license our name at that point, it did seem to us to represent a good opportunity.

We were a very young company, still located at 80 West 40th Street, when we were approached by a licensing broker about a Japanese department store that wanted to produce Liz Claiborne merchandise in Japan for the Japanese consumer. They would pay us a royalty on everything they sold, and our only obligation would be to provide them with samples of the clothing we were making, and they would pay us for that as well. They would be responsible for everything else: fabric, manufacturing, marketing, and then they would send us a check. It sounded too easy and too good to be true. But our company was just beginning, and it seemed like the arrangement could earn us a nice income stream with very little effort on our part.

Well, like many things, it was too good to be true. We had to do an enormous amount of work for what ended up being an inadequate return for our time and effort. Since the Japanese company was buying their own fabric, Liz had to approve their versions of the fabric we were using. And she also had to approve the colors, to make sure they coincided with our own. Fabrics, samples, and a thousand other items kept going back and forth between us in the States and our licensee in Japan for changes and approvals.

The handbags that propelled our accessories division.

With all of that, we also realized we didn't know enough about the marketing system in Japan. There, manufacturers virtually loaned the merchandise to the retailers, paying for everything including sales people and even guaranteeing the sale, so that if there was any merchandise left over, they had to take it back. In order to operate in this environment, manufacturers built in a huge markup, so that a skirt we might price to retail for $50 would sell for over $100 in Japan. It was almost shameful.

We weren't happy with the financial results, and we weren't happy with the quality of the product that the licensee produced.

We were forced to put up with this arrangement until the licensing agreement expired, and we certainly didn't renew. The experience taught us a lesson that would influence our arrangement with every other potential licensee: *once bitten twice shy*. Granting a license is at least as important as making a product inside your own company, and it needs to be managed as a part of the company. Once you give people carte blanche to do what they want to do with your label, then you're the fool. We became very, very careful about signing these agreements, making sure we only selected companies that could make an important and valuable contribution. We insisted on a close relationship with the licensee and controls so that whatever we were trying to accomplish got done the right way for our company and our consumer.

With all of that experience behind us we still ran into problems, and our first shoe license is a perfect example of that.

In 1982, we signed a licensing agreement with the US Shoe Corporation to manufacture a line of Liz Claiborne shoes. Our subsequent performance in the shoe area was good initially, but we ran into problems with US Shoe that were similar in a way to the problems we had with the Limited some years before.

Our arrangement was to manufacture shoes designed to be worn with the Liz Claiborne line of clothes for work. We were, however, already experiencing enormous growth in the Liz Sport division and felt that we should start taking advantage of the trend in sport shoes or sneakers, being led at that time by Nike. We felt that a Liz sneaker could be a home run. We tried to work with the folks at US Shoe to develop a line of appropriate shoes, but they kept dragging their feet. Nothing much got done, and we eventually discovered the reason – they really wanted the sport shoe business for themselves. The discovery soured our relationship to the point that we did not renew our license arrangement with them.

We were still a relatively small company, and we were growing so quickly, and consumers had such faith in our name that we wanted to make sure that any products we were associated with would be a positive for consumers and for retailers. We wanted to make sure that the companies we were doing business with had our best interests at heart. We wanted our own team at the licensee company devoted to Liz Claiborne exclusively, and we tried to put as many conditions into our arrangements as we could that would guarantee a good working relationship and a quality product. With all of this knowledge, we started discussions with an accessories company.

During the same period in 1982, we were approached by a young lady named Nina McLemore, who at the time was working for a company called Kayser-Roth. Kayser-Roth was a relic of the hosiery/lingerie world, and they'd also made some other items like gloves and socks. It had been bought and sold many times and was now a hodgepodge of businesses. It was part of a conglomerate parented by Gulf and Western Industries.

Nina came to see us with some ideas for a licensing arrangement between her company and ours. Having been a buyer and merchandise manager, she was well aware of the strength and the phenomenal success of Liz Claiborne. She said, "You know, the same consumer who is buying your sportswear also buys accessories. Why not take advantage of the Liz Claiborne name and make the kind of accessories that your consumer would love – handbags, scarves, all kinds of small leather goods? Accessories are a huge business and a Liz line of accessories would stimulate that consumer. The fact that they would be Liz Claiborne products would tell the consumer that they are well made and are offered at a good price. It certainly makes sense to us at Kayser-Roth."

It made sense to us at Liz, as well.

With tough conditions in place to protect our interests, we went into the accessory business with Kayser-Roth.

We worked very closely with Nina McLemore and her people, and Liz personally approved all the designs. Nothing could be put into work without her approval. At the same time, we would put our marketing strength behind the product to sell a new group of buyers at a completely different store location.

By this time in 1982, our logo had become extremely popular. Nina and her staff took the logo and designed a handbag that was made of vinyl but looked for all the world like leather. The bag was completely covered with images of small triangles and so told the world that the woman carrying the bag was a Liz Claiborne consumer. Was the design brand new and original, or were we paying homage to Louis Vuitton? It didn't matter. It was all Liz, and that bag became a runaway bestseller in every department store in America. Everybody had to have a Liz Claiborne bag with that logo. The logo design was used to great effect on other bags and accessories as well.

The accessories company itself kept enlarging its total offering to the market to include many other kinds of bags, some in vinyl but mostly in leather, along with belts and scarves. By 1985, the Kayser-Roth group had exited all its other business and was making Liz products exclusively. For all practical purposes, it was a Liz Claiborne company, even though we of course didn't own it and it retained the Kayser-Roth name.

The good news was that the accessory business was doing very well. The bad news was that the royalty income represented a very minor part of the total profit we could have been making if we *owned* the accessory company. We would have loved to buy the division from Kayser-Roth instead of just going along with the licensing arrangement. As we were starting to think about opening up the issues with them, a situation arose that turned into the opportunity of a lifetime and more than solved the problem.

Our licensing arrangement with K-R was very well written from our point of view. Our attorney, Ken Kopelman, from the Kramer Levin firm, had put together an agreement that protected us if a change of control were to take place at Kayser-Roth. Basically, they couldn't sell their company without our approval. This was only good business. After all, we were partners with them in a flourishing enterprise, and we could only imagine what would happen if, for example, they sold their company to a Liz Claiborne competitor. Our accessory business could be in deep trouble.

Here's where it gets interesting. K-R was a very small part of a much larger division that was a subsidiary of the Gulf and Western Industries, the sprawling conglomerate built by the legendary wheeler-dealer Charles Bluhdorn. The division, run by a fine gentleman named Jim Spiegel, consisted mainly of mattress companies and other assorted businesses and totaled close to $1 billion in volume. Our little piece of the pie at K-R / G & W was only doing about $50 million in 1985 when all this took place.

Sure enough, Gulf and Western Industries decided to get rid of the division which included our accessories business, and they made a deal with the

Wickes Company in Seattle. It was a big, billion dollar transaction, with Kayser-Roth only a tiny piece of the deal.

The discussions between G & W and Wickes went on for weeks, as they tried to settle all the points. They seem to have missed the change of control approval clause in our contract. At the last moment, virtually the day before the final papers were to be signed, the lawyers realized that they needed our approval or the whole deal would not go through. It was then that I received a call from Jim Spiegel. After some pleasantries, Jim said, "Jerry, I want to come over and see you. There's just a little technical thing that I wanted to talk to you about."

Of course I knew what was happening, and our lawyers knew what was happening. I suppose Jim was hoping we didn't.

He came by and said, "I was supposed to get you to sign this piece of paper, and with everything going on, somehow it got lost in the shuffle. I just need you to sign this saying that you agree with the sale that we're making."

"Jim," I said, "we don't agree. Frankly, we don't like the Wickes people. We don't think that the Wickes people have the vaguest idea of how to run an accessory division. We don't want our business to be in their hands."

He was absolutely flabbergasted. Of course he couldn't let the $50 million business interfere with his $1 billion deal, so he said, "What do you want to do?"

I was ready with an answer. "We'll take it off your hands."

"What do you mean you'll 'take it off our hands'?"

"Well, come up with a price that we both think is reasonable, and we'll buy the accessories division. We'll do it today."

They had to get their deal signed, so they had to accept our price. From our point of view, it had to be the bargain of the century. And the moral of the story is: *read agreements carefully before you sign them and remember what you agree to!*

This happened in 1985, and now we *owned* the accessory business. We brought the Kayser people in house to our headquarter building at 1441 Broadway where we now occupied perhaps 10 or 12 floors, having grown from just a half floor in a few short years. Their growth accelerated as the company became a leader in all of the individual accessories areas: handbags, small leather goods, scarves and belts. In 1988 we introduced Liz Claiborne jewelry, which in turn did extremely well. By 1989, the business had grown past $167 million, and we became the largest accessory company in the country.

Carol Hochman: Recollections of the Accessories Business

After the acquisition we moved to 1441 and spread our wings. We finally had a decent show room and the ability to add to staff. We became part of the corporation and began to share more with our sister divisions. We organized the business to make sure we allowed each classification to grow to be the number 1, 2 or 3 in its arena. We did this by setting up nuclear groups around the merchandiser who in effect became the "president" of Liz Claiborne Scarves or Liz Claiborne Belts, the thought being that if Echo Scarves, then the largest scarf producer, had people who just focused all day on building their business we needed to have that as well or we would never achieve our goals.

Sometime in the late 1980s we also began building Handbag and small leather goods shops in the major department stores. The shops insured our floor space and allowed us to make sure our goods were properly presented. They also increased volume significantly.

Late in 1988 or 1989 we introduced Liz Claiborne Jewelry. The stores were so on board with the success of accessories that they all go strongly behind this concept. Monet suddenly had a key competitor!

With the success of accessories, licensing became more interesting to us. Now we felt we knew how to do it right, and we embarked on a careful program of increasing the number of our licensees, but making sure we were protected with all of the restrictions and controls we've been talking about.

We went on to sign a handful agreements with other companies to manufacture hosiery and then home domestics such as sheets and pillowcases.

With hosiery, we felt the Liz Claiborne label would lift the products out of the commodity category, and we were right. It was very successful. With domestics, we thought we could make use of the wonderful prints in our line that could go on sheets and pillow cases.

We finally realized that we needed a coordinator who would spend full time overseeing our licensees, fielding all of their questions and handling the day-to-day responsibilities. We searched for a long time and finally hired Mary Belle, who joined the company in 1986, and who professionalized all of the licensing activities. We were now producing shoes, hosiery, and eyewear, including Liz Claiborne sunglasses, and we even got into Liz Claiborne frames for prescription glasses.

Even though Mary Belle was working diligently with our many licensees, Liz herself remained the tastemaker for all licensed merchandise, adding this task to the rest of her many design responsibilities. As I think back now, I realize how time consuming it was all becoming for Liz. She was busier than ever, and I remember how difficult it was even to plan a meeting with her as there never seemed to be enough hours in her day. She didn't seem to be enjoying herself much, but she did the job. She was a real trouper, but I've come to believe that little by little the job became for her less pleasure and more pain.

The involvement in the license-businesses also took time from our sales and marketing people who had to work on making sure the licensed product was not being shown in bits and pieces but rather made a substantial presentation that signified its importance to the store and its relevance to the consumer. I injected myself into this process, especially at the beginning, to make sure that the culture of our company was understood by the outside people making these products. I was very concerned that the Liz label not be tarnished in any way. I think we did a good job.

In the early 1980s, something else was happening in the apparel business: Jeans were becoming an important promotional category in the department stores. The business was dominated by Calvin Klein jeans at $29.95, and it represented one of the first forays by a true designer company into a popular priced product category. The combination of the designer name, and the fact that jeans were becoming acceptable daytime apparel, made this a big and growing business. Stores were having a difficult time getting the quantities they needed and were supplementing their Calvins with the product of other companies, including another iconic name, Gloria Vanderbilt.

Jerome A. Chazen

LIFE

RESCUING WHALES
OFF NEWFOUNDLAND

LINCOLN'S GREAT
DAY AT GETTYSBURG

CRIMINAL JUSTICE
IN CRISIS: PART 1

October 1983/$2.00

NANCY
REAGAN,
FIRST
RANCH
LADY

AN EXCLUSIVE VISIT AT
RANCHO DEL CIELO

Nancy Reagan in Liz denim — logo on shirt pocket.

We decided that women should be able to buy jeans from Liz Claiborne. We put a pair of jeans on our Liz Sport line, and the consumer, true to her feeling about Liz and our wonderful pant fit, bought them as fast as we could ship them. That seemed to us evidence that we could participate in this market in a big way. Despite the concern of the retailers, we insisted that our jeans could only be sold in the Liz departments of their stores. We did not want to be one more jean in the highly promotional denim area.

Our strategy worked. Almost overnight we became a major player in this world of denim. We made a variety of jean bottoms, but also expanded into an assortment of "denim appropriate styles" including jackets and a wonderful selection of tops to go with the jeans. This differentiated us from the major jean suppliers, who made only bottoms.

Everyone wore our denims. One day in October of 1983, someone came into our offices with a copy of the latest issue of *Life* Magazine. Pictured on the cover was First Lady Nancy Reagan, sitting on a rocking horse and wearing a pair of jeans and a very light denim blouse. In full view of millions of readers was our very own logo – the Liz Claiborne triangle. The wife of the President of the United States was wearing our denim! It was a wonderful moment, and we tried to take full advantage of this unintentional product endorsement.

Our denim sales were so strong that in 1985 we set up an entire division to take advantage of it. We created a new label for the products called Lizwear. Again, because of the reception our line got from the consumer, we were able to convince the department stores to give us separate open-to-buy and yet another department number.

Having a department gave us a huge advantage. If the consumer wanted a top to go with her jeans, we had them for her right there in the Lizwear department. She could buy a whole denim outfit if she wanted to without ever having to walk to another area of the store. It also kept us out of the denim area, where it seemed like price was the only factor driving sales. Our Liz denim departments became extremely profitable areas for the stores, selling our product at full price.

As I'm writing about all of this expansion that was taking place at Liz Claiborne, it occurs to me that some readers might wonder why we just couldn't keep producing the kinds of clothing that had worked for us instead of constantly looking for new areas of business to get into. I've thought a lot about this in the years since I left the company. On the one hand we seemed to be riding this wonderful wave, and we could have stayed where we were, enjoyed our success, and continued to offer our Liz Claiborne label goods to these wonderful Lizzies who believed in us. On the other hand, I just couldn't help thinking that the company should grow – that we should take advantage of all the things we had going for us and increase our volume as much as we possibly could. Just crossing the $100 million mark was an incredible achievement – and to think we went from there to considering that we could hit $1 billion! These were numbers never before reached in the fashion business, and I wanted us to get there. I think I was driven to keep that growth going.

As we thought about other categories of merchandise and other consumers we could bring into the Liz family, we began talking about one major group we had neglected – men. But *Liz Claiborne*, a *woman's* name on men's clothing? It didn't seem to make much sense. We began to look into the world of men's apparel in the department stores, and we came up with a very interesting statistic: over 50% of men's apparel, particularly in the sportswear area, was bought by women. It was the wives or the girlfriends picking out and purchasing clothing for their husbands or significant others. Sometimes the man was there with her in the store, but oftentimes he wasn't. This gave us a huge advantage because, of course, women were very familiar with our company.

We didn't think men would be comfortable wearing a shirt or sweater with a "Liz Claiborne" label on it. So we decided to call it just "Claiborne." We discussed the concept with the stores, telling them that we wanted to put together a men's sportswear line that mirrored to some degree what we had done in women's. We weren't looking to re-invent the world, but just make things that men would like to wear. We started the division in 1985, and we brought in Jay Margolis, a young but veteran menswear executive to run it. All of us, especially Liz, were impressed with Jay's knowledge of the industry and his appreciation for the Liz name and what it could mean in menswear. Jay had the responsibility of hiring a completely new staff of designers, merchandisers, and even patternmakers – we wanted to do it right. We saw ourselves as a slightly lower-price Ralph Lauren, as always taking advantage of our overseas production expertise to bring prices down without hurting the quality of the goods.

While we were previewing our first line, we invited some principals of the retailing world to take a look. David Farrell, the CEO of the May Company, came up to inspect our new goods. David was very much a hands-on manager – more than any other top executive that we did business with.

Dave's visits to his branches were legendary. He would zero in on the smallest details of his managers' businesses. It was scary how well he knew every detail. He might question one of his merchants: "How come your hosiery business isn't up to par?" "Why is it that your women's sportswear business, which was running 14% ahead of plan, is all of a sudden 4% down? What's going on there?" He knew all of the facts about their businesses. When they'd walk through the stores together, David would question every fixture, every display. "How do you expect to sell this jacket if this is the way you show it?" His managers knew that when David Farrell came to town, they were in for a rough time.

Well, he came up to our showroom and he wanted to see what our men's product was going to look like. His company, the May company, did hundreds of millions of dollars worth of men's business, and we wanted him to see how the Liz Claiborne magic would work in mens'. Jay Margolis (a staff salesperson wouldn't do) showed him the merchandise, as I watched from afar.

David didn't pull his punches. Well," he said, "It's interesting, but I don't think you belong in the men's business."

I took a quick look to see if he was joking, but he had a serious look on his face.

"Really?" I replied. "You know, we've been getting a pretty good feeling from other retailers. They seem to like it. They think there's a place for us in this part of the business. Can you tell me why you feel this way?"

"You're too expensive."

We were all shocked. We had worked so hard to pack designer fabrics and details into the product.

He explained, "You know, men don't buy pants the way women buy pants." He pointed to one of the items. "You've got a pant here that's $40 retail. It's not worth it. I can walk into a store and buy the same pant for $32 retail. Why would anybody pay $40?"

He went on basically attacking our pricing structure and telling us that even though we thought we were giving good value with our better fabrics and high quality manufacturing, it just didn't appeal to him.

After more discussion, he said, "It's not going to work, but we'll try it. But I know it's not going to work."

He was partly right. The problem was that many of the May branches appealed to a somewhat down-market consumer, well below the level of

Macy's or Bloomingdale's. We knew that Ralph Lauren refused to sell to many of the May branches for that very reason. But the men's merchandise did work for our other customers, and the division became very successful. Jay certainly participated in that success, and eventually he moved into bigger jobs in the women's area at our company.

I mentioned earlier the Estee Lauder challenge that we used for goal-setting in our company. That had some unintended but very positive consequences for Liz Claiborne. As we studied the way in which Estee Lauder came to dominate its market, we learned about the fragrance and cosmetics business. Using our own staff, we did quite a bit of research into the industry and found that virtually every important European designer and a number of American designers were involved in fragrance. In most cases, these companies licensed their name to fragrance companies and lived on the royalties. With our philosophy about organic growth and the fact that Liz Claiborne had a special consumer following, we thought we should start our own company.

We met with Jim Preston, the CEO of Avon Products, and we liked what he had to say, so in December, 1985, we entered into a 50% owned joint venture partnership with them that we called Liz Claiborne Cosmetics. Avon became our supplier, and we took the sales and marketing end of the business.

The following year, through the good offices of Avon, we were led to the people of IFF, International Flavors and Fragrance, who were going to develop our first perfume. The process was like nothing we had ever encountered before. The IFF people interviewed Liz to talk about the things that she was most interested in, how she led her life, her extracurricular activities, and other personal factors. The idea was that they would blend a fragrance that really represented Liz herself. This is how companies convince consumers that somehow or other the fragrance they are buying actually reflects the personality of some celebrity or other.

They went away and did their work. Then they came back and asked us to participate in a selection process as they had developed a number of fragrances they thought were appropriate, and they wanted Liz's feeling as to which one she liked the most. The funny part was that Liz had already told me that she really wasn't much of a fragrance person. She rarely if ever used fragrance, and it was certainly not an important part of her world the way pants were, for instance. But she did understand the corporate ramifications of having a fragrance and was more than willing to go along.

We are in the fragrance business.

Jerome A. Chazen

Liz asked me to accompany her to this – this sort of wine tasting for perfume. I think she thought I could provide her with some protection. At any rate, we entered a room with a lot people from IFF and Avon whom we didn't know sitting around a big table. There were also some professional perfume smellers present, known in their industry as "noses."

The group conducted a blind "smell test" (I'm sure they had a fancier name for it) featuring the fragrances they had developed plus others that were already on the market. Everyone sniffed each fragrance and they wrote down their comments.

I was there for Liz, but I started to sniff these things and I couldn't smell anything. One was just like the other to me. But the people from the industry were saying things like, "It has a hint of lilac but a very strong rose feeling. And daffodil is present and helping to lift the scent." You could have knocked me over with a feather. I had no idea what they were talking about. I wasn't getting any of those aromas. I kept thinking to myself, "Is this real? Are they actually sensing all those flavors?"

Apparently it was real, and it turned out that Liz had a pretty good nose and was able to appreciate the different smells and the variations in the fragrances. The one we ended up with was mostly Liz's pick, although some of the other people in the room were in on it.

IFF then tested this fragrance against "White Linen," the Estee Lauder fragrance that was the market leader, to see if people trying both would like ours better. They also wanted to make sure the two were different enough to give people a distinct choice. We did well in the tests and decided to enter the market with this particular fragrance, which we of course called Liz Claiborne.

Once we had the fragrance or "juice" as it's called in the industry, we needed a bottle to put it in. The glass container is an extremely important factor in building a perfume brand, and here I had some very strong feelings. My wife, Simona, and I had become very serious contemporary glass art collectors. I was fairly knowledgeable about what could be done with glass design, and I wanted our perfume bottle to be outstanding. We had one designed that reflected the look of our triangle logo.

We did find the fragrance business to be different from the apparel business in every way imaginable. When we did our original research, the elements of the business became very clear: Raw materials were the least important cost element to be concerned with. I know it's shocking to most people who buy these very expensive products, but the actual cost of the perfume is very small. Most of the costs come with the packaging, advertising, and marketing.

We ran the numbers very carefully and looked at all of the elements we would have to deal with. It seemed to us that they approached the product in a completely opposite way. We tried to pack as much value as we could into our garments, and now we had to create value with hype.

We brought in a brilliant executive named Wendy Banks as VP of Marketing to work with us on it. For the first time in the company's history, we had to hire advertising agencies that would create campaigns for the fragrances. In addition, we had to hire and pay our own salespeople to work behind the fragrance counters in the department stores. In all, we had to shoulder far more of the responsibility for selling to the consumer at the retail level than in the apparel business. We knew this would be the case going in. And since we wanted to be in the fragrance business, so be it.

Our plan worked and we became a major player in the fragrance industry, developing additional perfumes and colognes over the years. We started shipments in late 1986 and in 1987 our sales reached $26 million. By the end of 1987, a trade publication named Liz Claiborne one of the top five brands of perfume. In 1988 we quickly reached $44 million in sales; $60 million in 1989; $72 million in 1990. While fragrance wasn't a huge business for us, we felt that it would be an important business and one that would help the credibility and fashion significance of the company, which it did.

A couple of years after getting into this market, our business partner, Avon, bought a company that had several different fragrance labels of its own. Our agreement with Avon forbade this, as we wanted to make sure we were exclusive with them. As a result, in 1988 we were able to buy them out, and we became the sole owners of our perfume division.

Where to look next for growth?

In 1987, we began to look up – upwards to higher priced garments as the next area we wanted to move into. Liz Claiborne was in what is known as the "better" price category – the largest and most important one in the department stores. We were positioned above "moderate" but below

125

"bridge." Above bridge was the highest price group of all – the designer labels.

We started to think about making this move by taking Liz from being a "better" line and coming up with some Liz product that would move us into the "bridge" area, which was growing rapidly in the stores.

The biggest player in the bridge area at the time was Ellen Tracy. Ellen Tracy had made the move from being a better sportswear manufacturer to the bridge area, and had done it very successfully. Of course their volume was very small compared to ours. But they were doing a good job with stores like Neiman Marcus, Saks, and Bloomingdale's, which had the most significant bridge departments.

As we discussed this internally, we came to feel that it would be very difficult to take the Liz line and simply make it more expensive by upgrading the fabrics we were using.

We thought we would probably lose many of the consumers who depended on our merchandise because they couldn't afford to move up to bridge prices. By the same token, the typical bridge customer would look upon a Liz Claiborne offering and think, "It's just the same Liz Claiborne clothes, and now they're trying to get more money for it."

Heavy merchandise discussion- Jerry & Liz.

So we decided that if we wanted to enter the bridge business we should do it under another name and with a new line that didn't have any association with Liz, at least in the eyes of the consumer. It never occurred to us to buy an existing bridge company just to add it to our portfolio as other companies might have done. We knew we had the manufacturing facilities to produce this merchandise. We certainly had the textile knowledge to go out and buy more expensive fabrics. And we felt sure that we could come up with the right kind of design spirit to make the line attractive and compelling. But we needed a name and a label.

Liz felt very strongly that a member of her design team and a very important associate of hers, Dana Buchman, could move into the position of being the head of the bridge division and have the privilege of her name on the label as well.

Dana had joined the company to work on knitwear, and she had become Liz's favorite knitwear designer. The intricacies of sweater design require a lot of specialized skills and knowledge that Liz herself didn't have, so she came to appreciate what Dana brought to our company. Dana became a key contributor not only in knitwear but for all woven garments throughout our collection. She also acted as a second pair of eyes for Liz over the design of the line generally. Their relationship grew stronger over the years, and Liz placed more and more confidence in her.

So here again, as when we started Liz, we had a company with a real person – a real designer – on the label and as the face of the company for consumers. We introduced the line into the stores in 1987 in the fall season. We didn't anticipate it being a giant business because the bridge business itself was not that large. Prior to her leaving the company in 1989, Liz did of course oversee the Buchman line designs. Dana Buchman showed nice growth, with sales going from $5.6 million in 1987 to $73.5 million in 1992. The division became an important part of the bridge category for some department stores. We tried to keep pace with the volume that Ellen Tracy was doing, and while I don't think we ever exceeded it, we came very close.

During this decade of rapid growth and success followed by more success, Liz, as I mentioned earlier, was not entirely content. As we became a larger organization with a vast number of employees and many lines of apparel to oversee, her designing time was cut down to almost zero. Money, fame, the satisfaction of building a great company – none of these things held any real appeal for her. She accepted what was happening, the transformation from a small shop to a major corporation, and she worked hard to make it happen, but I know she did not delight in it.

She found it difficult even to supervise other designers, hating to have to tell someone that their work wasn't good. In fact, someone else had to do it for her. In a sense the success of the company took away the thing she loved most, sitting at her table and designing her garments.

But through it all she was a trouper and never let people see her discomfort even as her fame grew and the demands of the business required her to make public appearances.

The department stores had begun approaching us with ideas for events that would include in-store fashion shows with Liz on hand to mingle with customers, discuss the merchandise and advise them on what to buy. I thought it was a fabulous idea, as it distinguished us from every other manufacturer out there. Nobody in our price category had ever done anything like this.

One day I got a telephone call from Jim Nordstrom. He was the CEO of a regional department store chain headquartered in Seattle. The store had a presence in the Northwest, having grown from being a shoe store decades earlier to a viable retail operation. Their uniqueness lay in their focus on customer service. As we had known, the company was opening a store in Salt Lake City – their buyers had been to the showroom and ordered a lot of Liz Claiborne merchandise for the opening. Now Jim was calling to invite Liz herself to the opening. His thought was that while few people in Utah had heard of Nordstrom's at that time, *everybody* knew Liz. Liz agreed to visit the Salt Lake City store, and she was the star of the opening. Her appearance was a major contributor to the store's success, and the event cemented our relationship with Nordstrom's and the Nordstrom family for many years to come.

In spite of the demand for them, these public appearances or PAs as we called them were few and far between simply because Liz didn't like doing them. They embarrassed her. She was a shy, private person, and she didn't like being the center of attention that way. Whenever she did accept an invitation, I always accompanied her just to support her.

During our really heady growth years, the demand was so great that she could have spent half her time doing PAs. The stores loved the events and there is no question in my mind that they strengthened the relationship between the consumer and our company. They helped create our world of Lizzies, the literally millions of women who swore by Liz Claiborne merchandise. These women bought our merchandise, loved it, loved the quality, loved the prices and loved Liz. And when they saw her at PAs, they let her know it. They treated her like a rock star.

I'll never forget one day we had a PA planned in Denver, Colorado. Because of weather problems, our flight was many hours late. Liz was supposed to be in the department store at three o'clock in the afternoon, but we didn't even get to Denver until seven in the evening. It was a bad situation and we felt terrible about it. The store had someone waiting for us at the airport, and when we met up with the person, he said, "We've got to get you to the store right away."

All I could do was apologize profusely, "We're sorry, we're so sorry. We feel terrible for all those people who showed up to see Liz."

His response astonished me. "The people are still there. They haven't left the store. And they want to see Liz. Please, let's hurry."

We arrived at the store and a huge cheer went up when Liz walked into the department. She was a celebrity to these women. And there was Liz still huffing and puffing and trying to recover from the arduous travel day. She collected herself and did her usual outstanding show that I think gave the department one of the biggest volume days in its history. It was an experience I'll never forget.

We were growing like topsy, but we weren't growing by trying to sell the same consumer more of the same. We were growing by giving her a greater variety of product and trying to take care of all her needs. It was legitimate, natural growth. We weren't trying to buy growth through acquisitions. That just wasn't our style. Even without that kind of artificial bottom line booster, we were on our way to becoming the largest fashion apparel company in the world.

In 1988 we began to discuss yet another consumer we could serve – the larger size woman. Our Misses product was manufactured in sizes 4 to 14. When we started researching the American consumer, we found that almost 50 percent of women wore larger sizes. Once we recognized the extent of this market and the fact that this consumer was being underserved in the department stores, we felt that it was an area ripe for development. At the same time, our prime account, Saks Fifth Avenue, told us about their own research: consumers were unhappy that Saks did not carry apparel in their size range.

The opportunity was obvious. But I have to say we worried a bit and wondered whether we wanted our designs to be shown in these larger sizes – what would it do to our image and our fashion influence? We thought about it and finally concluded, "Well, why not? Why shouldn't we take care of that lady?" In a way we were also saying, "If it's good enough for Saks, it's good enough for Liz Claiborne." So we were off again, starting yet another division, which we called "Elisabeth." The retailers across the country were pleased. They welcomed our participation in this market, and we became the backbone of the large size sportswear departments, and our Elisabeth division prospered.

Linda Larsen: On Elisabeth

In the fall of 1988 I was called to the boardroom and told that I was to be promoted to president of the new large size women's division. I was ready for the task. It was a tremendous thrill and honor to be the first employee to have come up through the ranks of the company and be chosen president and creative director of a new product line within Liz Claiborne.

Within weeks we decided to use Liz's full name, Elisabeth, for the brand, and we were on the way to creating another new business for the company. We had a dedicated and talented design team, our own production team and our own fit model, a perfect size 18 from day one! We soon added a marketing and sales team.

Elisabeth was the first designer, large size collection in the marketplace. There was no existing business or marketing model to follow, but we had the strength of the Liz Claiborne method to guide us. We chose to dress our new consumer exclusively instead of "sizing up" from the missy collection. The starting point was "our lady" and she was always in our minds, first and foremost. Our approach provided us with a unique designer collection that entered the retail world just as the "special size" consumer was finally being recognized by department stores.

In so many ways we honored this woman who had been searching for fashion in her size. Incorporating new fabrics and prints that would accent her form, we utilized the standards and philosophies of Liz Claiborne: we sold our seasonal offerings as a collection, designed the line so that it was easy to make outfits with versatility, offered well priced items in color multipliers and merchandised with intent to show a "store within a store concept."

It was an incredibly busy time: There were fashion shows and new shop openings. I traveled country wide to visit stores, meeting and listening to consumers. The business grew rapidly starting with a select 100 "doors" in top branches across the country. Monitoring growth and holding back in the start up phase was difficult. Store presidents campaigned for more doors, and for a time, I was the most popular gal in town!

I had the honor of representing the company in many Elisabeth Shop openings across the country and met hundreds if not thousands of customers. Women who would hug me and thank me for bringing them fashion in their size. They all told me to bring this message home: "Thanks LIZ!"

In 1992 the company opened its first free standing Elisabeth store at Tyson's Corner Mall in Atlanta.

We listened to the marketplace, created a product our new consumer loved, and right out of the box the Elisabeth product was a great success and demand was incredible, from both consumers and retail stores alike. Within three years Elisabeth grew to be a $250 million dollar business occupying two floors of its own at 1441 Broadway.

We didn't stop there. We found yet another clothing category that was being merchandised separately in the stores and that we really weren't representing fully enough in the Liz Claiborne product line: knitwear. Consumers were falling in love with everything knitted: knitted pants, knitted skirts, knitted jackets, and knitted tops of all kinds. There were already manufacturers doing extremely well selling knit apparel, and we decided to join the fray. In 1989, we opened another division called Liz & Company to be entirely devoted to knitwear. This line was shown in the knit areas of the department stores. While it never became a huge business, it was a very good and profitable business and one that we liked a lot.

1989 was a watershed year for the company. We had been in business for a little more than a decade and achieved success by any measure, when two of the original founders decided to retire.

By this time, Liz had become an icon. The press coverage, the public appearances, the amazing success of the company turned her into a reluctant rock star of sorts. Many people in and out of the business, especially young designers joining the company, were in awe of her and her legend.

As the company grew larger and larger, Liz's influence on it had changed. She was no longer doing day-to-day designing, but instead was kind of an overseer of the designs coming out of all the company's divisions. She would participate in design meetings to give her blessing to the product.

For a couple of years prior to her departure, Liz and Art had been taking more and more time off from the business. First it was every Friday, then Thursdays as well. Art had fulfilled one of his dreams by buying an airplane that could take him and Liz anywhere anytime. They did quite a bit of traveling and bought property: a ranch in Montana, a home in St.Barts. At one point they came up with the idea of working one month, taking off the next month, and come back to work the next. The arrangement, which seemed ridiculous at the outset, proved impossible to live with. So in some ways their leaving the company was a relief.

There was certainly an impact on our people, but in fact the void Liz left was psychological rather than practical. There were people in place doing all the work, and the work continued.

The same thing was true of Art, who was retiring with her. While he had not backed away entirely from the responsibilities of overseeing aspects of the overseas manufacturing work and being involved in fabrics, there were plenty of people qualified to take over his duties.

For a long while I had felt that the growth of the company was as much my doing as Liz's, and maybe more mine than hers. I know this will sound ungenerous, but I believed then and still believe now that whatever success Liz and Art might have had on their own, it would never have been anything like what we accomplished together.

I don't want to take anything away from Liz's design abilities, her uncanny understanding of a certain consumer's needs, and her exquisite good taste.

But I did feel for many years that the direction and growth of the company was principally my doing. Yet at that time I didn't have the title, and I never had the public recognition or credit.

Liz was nominally president and CEO. In actuality, she never performed the duties of those offices. The press, however, because of the excitement of a woman presiding over a Fortune 500 company, made the most of her involvement and success. Their articles emphasized that she had built the business – done it all – with the help of her husband, Art. It was agonizing to read these kinds of stories about our company and never see my name mentioned.

Much of this was due to Art. As appreciative as he was at the very beginning when we were forming the company, now, after all the success we had enjoyed, he couldn't be generous and acknowledge what I had meant to it. Maybe it was a matter of keeping it all for Liz, or payback for the strains in our relationship that had existed since college. Art had never had been as comfortable in the business as Liz, Leonard, and I had. In a way, we were naturals at what we did and enjoyed our individual roles tremendously. I never observed those kinds of feelings in Art, and maybe he resented seeing them in us. Well, it's hard to speculate.

I always felt that Liz was an innocent bystander to Art's machinations. She was always very supportive of him when it came to his relationship with me. But I have to say with gratitude that my personal relationship with Liz never faltered. I appreciated what she did for the company, and she appreciated what I did. I don't think it would be wrong to say it was our company – Liz's and Jerry's. At least that's the way I like to think of it now.

There was a lot of press coverage of Liz and Art's departure. It was big news. Interestingly, there was rarely a mention of me and my role in the history and success of the company. The "founders" were leaving, and that was that.

In truth, one of the founders was still there. And over the years the financial community not only considered me the face of the company but also its driving force. I did receive an enormous amount of good press from the Wall Street analysts covering Liz Claiborne. On the other hand, Woman's Wear Daily and Vogue never gave up the fiction that it was *all Liz* with some help from Art.

But, at last, I did become chairman and CEO of our great company.

133

After the departure of Liz and Art, all of our divisions continued to grow, and all of our growth came from within. The question became: where can we go now? How can we sustain this growth in the future? We were so completely dominant in the better apparel market, with such a huge share of market that it seemed unlikely our growth rate could continue, especially since the department stores were no longer expanding. The future was not going to be easy.

I sensed that the next opportunity for the company was in the enormous, lower-priced apparel market, and we had to figure out a way to get into it. We knew that we did not want to use any Liz Claiborne labels on low-priced merchandise. We didn't want consumers to think that they could now buy the same Liz products for less money. We needed to come up with a good product line, probably of somewhat lesser quality, using lower grade fabric, but that still offered consumers in this market better value and taste than our competitors. And we had to match our competitors' prices. We did a lot of investigating and checked with many of our factories overseas and we concluded that we could do it.

Now we needed a label for this merchandise that had nothing to do with Liz Claiborne, although using a label that was already recognizable to consumers would give us a leg up.

As luck would have it, in 1992, three very good labels that had operated in this part of the market became available. An old low-end manufacturer called Russ Togs Inc was in trouble and headed for bankruptcy. Not only did they own the Russ label, but they owned the "Villager" and "Crazy Horse" labels as well. In all, they were good vehicles for us to use to enter what was called the "moderate" area of the department stores, and we acquired these names in 1992. The plan was for the Russ label to feature career and casual clothing for department stores; Villager would be about office apparel with some casual mixed in and sold at Kohl's; and we would use Crazy Horse for contemporary sportswear, again, in department stores.

The head merchandiser at Kohl's was a gentleman named Jay Baker. I had known Jay for years, from the time he was a department store buyer. He had been a buyer and merchandiser for Saks, the head of a short-lived Saks specialty store venture called Thimbles, and was now presiding over Kohl's, a fast growing, free standing specialty operation. I thought Villager would be a natural for Kohl's.

We invited Jay into the showroom, discussed the concept with him, and decided to give them the Villager label exclusively. In return we received favorable floor position and quantity orders. The Kohl's growth, which continues to this day, was almost like the Liz growth in its early years, and Villager went along for the ride.

In three years – 1994 – the moderate division reached a high point in sales of $111.6 million.

The decade that began with our initial public offering 1981 was, as I hope I've conveyed, one of hard work, tremendous excitement, wonderful success, rapid growth, and for me, great personal satisfaction. I've already talked about our going public as a source of enormous pride because it meant that we were a serious, successful company worthy of investors' attention. But that was only the beginning.

In 1986 Liz Claiborne became a member of the Fortune 500; it had entered the rarified atmosphere of the largest and mightiest industrial companies in the country. Having begun life only eleven years earlier, it was one of the youngest companies ever to make the cut.

Simona Chazen, Mike Gould and myself

In 1991, we were honored to have our shares listed for the first time ever on the New York Stock Exchange. The company began trading under the symbol LIZ on February 20, of that year. A listing on the NYSE meant that we were recognized as a well-run, financially stable business making important contributions to the US Economy.

The sales numbers from across the decade attest to our achievement:

- At the end of 1981, the year we went public, our sales reached $116.8 million. Ten years later, at the end of 1991, annual sales rocketed past the $2 billion mark. Compare these results with our earliest sales -- $2 million in 1976; $23 million in 1978; $79 million in 1980.
- Net income went from $10.2 million to $222.7 million
- During that same ten year period, we grew from about 350 employees to 7,800.
- Earnings per share (on a split adjusted basis) moved from 8.25 cents to $2.61.
- Our share price tells a similar story: If you had purchased 1,000 shares of our stock at the initial offering price, it would have cost you $19,000. Ten years later, that investment was worth over $1,000,000.

Toward the end of this decade of growth, public recognition of our success began to pour in. In November of 1989, I received a wonderful letter from Marshall Loeb, then the editor of *Fortune* magazine, congratulating Liz Claiborne on being rated the most admired company in the entire apparel industry. When the issue January 29, 1990, issue of *Fortune* came out announcing this honor – well it was an unbelievable, indescribable feeling.

I felt the honor was so great because while it recognized our spectacular performance in the apparel marketplace, it also reflected the opinions of our peers – other top executives from top companies – as to the merits of Liz Claiborne. Industry executives, outside directors, and financial analysts rate the companies on eight attributes: quality of management, quality of products or services, innovativeness, long term investment value, financial soundness, ability to attract, develop and keep talented people, community and environmental responsibility, and use of corporate assets.

The following year, we earned even more honors from *Fortune* and our peers at the largest companies in the US. We became one of "America's

Most Admired Corporations," joining the list at #10. Now this was for *all* companies, not just apparel. And we continued to make the list in the two following years as well: we were #4 in the nation in the February, 1992, issue, and then #8 in 1993. I have to admit that I was also proud and delighted to have my picture appear two different times on *Fortune's* covers along with other top CEO's from other "most admired" companies.

If anything, these honors validated what we had built at Liz both financially and culturally for our customers, consumers, shareholders and employees. And again, it was the recognition by our peers that was probably most important, especially since this was occurring after three of the founders had left the company. (Leonard Boxer retired in 1985.) There was no question that the heights that we had reached as a company was due to the hard work of a lot of people.

It was a very heady time, and looking back at it now, it is remarkable how we were able to put together all of the elements that allowed us to make Liz Claiborne so successful. It was a combination of Liz and the design staff creating the right product for our consumer, our ever-growing production staff finding appropriate contractors in countries around the world, not only in the Far East, but in Central America, and even the Middle East. Obviously, we had the support of our main customers, the department stores, who where only too happy to work with us as we kept their cash registers ringing.

When I think of our achievements, I also see the growth of the vertical specialty store chain as a culmination of what we were doing: identifying a consumer and trying to own that consumer – taking care of all her clothing needs. That's exactly what the Gap, Abercrombie & Fitch, the Limited, and a whole host of other specialty stores try to do today.

A November, 1991 article in *Woman's Wear Magazine* ranked the four leading sportswear companies, noting they were responsible for an estimated $1.5 billion in wholesale sales: Liz Claiborne was at $970 million, Jones New York near $200 millions, JH Collectibles also near $200 million, and Evan Picone at about $125 million. (Interestingly, JH Collectibles was run by another very good friend and fraternity brother of mine from the University of Wisconsin, Ken Ross.)

Liz Claiborne's leadership position was clear. The other three companies had a head start – they had been around longer than us – but we zoomed past them and just kept going.

As far as our sales as a percentage of a store's volume goes – one of my pet goals and measures of success – the article mentioned a store called Younkers, where we hit an astonishing 7.6% of the total volume. I remember that moment, and I remember that I immediately started talking up a 10% goal, which, remarkably, we were able to achieve in many stores.

We had come a long, long way from the original 1% goal we had set at the beginning of the decade – our decade of unparalleled achievement.

Chapter 7

Everything's on Sale – All the Time

My friend Mike Gould is the long-time CEO of Bloomingdale's. When we first met in the early 1980s, Mike was general merchandise manager of Robinson's Department Stores in Los Angeles.

When he came to visit us in New York, Robinson's was already a substantial customer of ours and one of our most important outlets in southern California. As we were discussing our company's approach to the apparel business, he suddenly commented, "You know we buy a lot of merchandise from you. What happens if it doesn't sell?"

I looked at him and said, "Well, obviously not everything sells all the time. Sometimes there will be items you'll have to mark down."

He looked at me with a pained expression on his face and said, "Markdowns? What do you mean? If there are any markdowns, we certainly would expect you to help out, to participate in these markdowns."

What he was suggesting was that Liz should be ready to partner with Robinson's for the losses they'd incur by putting our merchandise on sale, as they would not be getting the full retail price they were counting on.

I was a little nonplussed, and I answered him rather bluntly. "Mr. Gould, each of us has a job. It's our job as a company to design and make the best possible product. It's your job to sell that product. And I don't think we want to be in each other's business."

Jerome A. Chazen

Fortune cover- Quite an accomplishment.

He laughed, and then I laughed, and we've been friends ever since.

I think of that encounter in these times of constant markdowns and what seem to be never-ending sales. Back then, selling your merchandise below the established retail price was serious business not to be taken lightly.

When I started in retailing in the 1950's, markdowns were, of course, necessary. They occurred when certain styles were slow selling, or they

140

involved merchandise at the end of the selling season, or there was damaged or shop worn merchandise to get rid of.

When the decision was made to take a markdown, an assistant or sometimes the buyer would have to go to the items in question, grab hold of the price tag, cross out the original printed price (usually with a red pencil), and physically write in the new markdown price. This had to be done on every single item included in the markdown. And once the new price was written in, it was there forever. Well, you could cross it out again and put in a lower price, but you could never raise it. For this reason, markdowns were carefully thought through, planned, and executed. They were like a rite of passage for inexperienced buyers.

The system was efficient, if old school. The buyer would have to keep track of how many prices were changed, enter them into a markdown book and then send it to the merchandising office so that the markdown activity from every department could be compiled. The management would be able to see just how many dollars worth of markdowns had been taken. This would affect the profitability of the department and, eventually, the profitability of the entire store. It was all very serious.

Technology drastically changed all that, made changing prices *up or down* very easy as I will explain, and created chaos in the industry. In fact, I would argue that it changed retail philosophy in unintended ways: from the judicious use of markdowns to get rid of slow selling merchandise to creative leveraging of price adjustments to increase sales.

The changes started with the idea someone had of identifying individual garments with a bar code printed on the ticket. Supermarkets did it first. Every product in the store was bar coded and then scanned when the customer checked out. The price of the item didn't even necessarily have to appear on the product, instead it would be displayed on the shelf where the product sat.

It was a battle at the beginning to get fashion people to apply this technique to their business. We were fashion companies with images and brands to protect, and we didn't want consumers thinking we were apparel supermarkets. But some of the larger retail chains started to insist that manufacturers add the bar codes because they saw it as a major time and money saver for themselves. Not only did manufacturers then have to get into the bar code business, but at around the same time stores insisted that we actually print and attach the price ticket to the merchandise, something vendors had never done before.

I wrote earlier in the book about how I would take stubs home to determine what had sold that day. The tickets that the stores put on the merchandise back then were two part tickets perforated in the center. When a garment was sold, the salesperson tore off half the ticket and put it into a little box where they were all collected. That's how the stores kept track of what items were sold.

With bar codes, no tickets were torn. Instead they were scanned and all of the information in the code went into the store's computer system, giving an exact tally of what had sold by style, size, color and so forth. Each evening, in a matter of minutes, management could get a tabulated account of the totals of all sales in all of their stores. It was a tremendous boon for the retailers, giving them information that used to take days and sometimes weeks to put together. So all of that was good.

I would venture to say that almost all of the new technological innovations have been helpful and saved both time and money. But there is this one exception, and that is the way this technology gave retailers the ability to program their computers so that merchandise could be re-priced at will. The item would be scanned at the register by the salesperson, and the new price would pop up.

Now retailers didn't have to go through the laborious process of changing the original price printed on the item's ticket. They could *raise or lower* prices and consumers would not see any evidence on the ticket. They would only see a sale sign over the merchandise. All price adjustments would be taken at the register. Retailers could remove the signs any time they wanted, punch a few keys on the computer and change the price once again – up or down.

It sounds kind of innocent, but the technology now enabled the stores to take spot markdowns instantly, any time they wanted, and that's where the problems began. It was so easy to run a sale, create excitement in the department and perhaps do a little extra business, then raise the price back up.

Retailers started to get very creative, shall we say, exercising this new freedom. They started using it to boost sales during slow periods. If business was crawling along on a particular Tuesday, it was possible for a merchant to print a sign that read "30% OFF," put the sign on a merchandise rack, and program the computer to charge the customer the new lower price.

It all seemed too good to be true and, of course, it was. The whole retail industry moved from this small beginning until there was a flood of sale signs in stores and almost no control over the cost of these markdowns, the cost of the dollars lost by not getting full price for the item. Again, I am not talking about traditional markdowns, but rather these price cuts designed to stimulate sales on brand new, fresh merchandise.

I saw this as a terrible way to sell. When it first started happening, I would sit down with store people and try to explain the problem to them, but they just didn't care. I would tell them that if they put out merchandise with a sign saying "20% OFF" or "40% OFF, the merchandise would be cherry picked by the consumer. She would take what she liked best and leave the rest. At the end of the day or two days, when the promotion was over, the store would raise the price back up on goods that no one wanted even at the special lower price!

Look at it from the consumer's perspective: she comes into the department and sees a whole rack of jackets with a sign saying "20% OFF." She picks out what she wants and so do fifty other customers. What's left? The leavings. Now the leavings in the old days would be marked down further because if people wouldn't buy them at 20% off, maybe they'll buy them at 40% off. But what was happening now was just the opposite: stores would mark the items back up to regular price and think they were going to sell. This logic never made any sense to me.

The stores were digging a deeper and deeper hole for themselves that they could never crawl out of. The promotional activity in the stores and the sale mentality among store managers increased dramatically. The number of markdowns rose and rose and rose as the years went on. The easiest way to generate some quick volume became running big promotional ads in the newspaper saying "Come in. All men's shirts are 20% off. Today only." So they'd get you in the store on that day, and then the following day they would take the sign off.

Maybe that was okay for a quick, short-term fix, but it became a long-term disaster. This practice, in effect, trained the consumer to wait for sales. Customers pretty quickly got very smart and began to say "Well, it was 20%

off yesterday, and I'm certainly not going to pay full price today. I'll wait a few days and it will be 20% off again – or maybe even more!"

The stores now had to keep having these sales and special promotions in order to bring in customers, and in the process, prices would be artificially lowered, and the merchandise devalued. The customer became a perpetual bargain hunter, and the retailers were on their way to becoming bargain stores with razor thin margins.

This focus on promotions was exacerbated by a concept the retailers embraced called "beat last year." Day by day sales records were being kept, and the object was to beat one-year-ago sales on any particular day. If a sales promotion had boosted sales say on July 18 *last year*, something had to be done to beat that number on July 18 *this year*. And how do you do that? You guessed it, another sale or special promotion. And so an unending, vicious circle was created.

When I got into this business, the whole idea was to sell quality merchandise at regular price – a fair price – to pay expenses and allow everybody to make a profit. That idea began to disappear, and profits along with it. The scramble for pennies began. In today's department stores, virtually nothing is sold at regular price anymore. Everything is on sale, all the time, even when it doesn't have to be.

Here's a personal "Mother's Day" shopping story to illustrate this point.

There is a large department store branch close to where I live in Rockland County, New York. Invariably, as Mother's Day approached, I would realize that I hadn't yet gotten a gift for my wife. Typically, on the day before Mother's Day, I would get myself over to the store to see if I could find an appropriate present. Over the years I had gotten into the habit of giving Simona a robe, so I headed for the lingerie department. The store was very crowded, as it usually is the day before Mother's Day, with lots of other shoppers making their last minute purchases. The department I was shopping in was extra busy because robes, pajamas, and nightgowns always serve well as Mother's Day gifts.

I spotted a large rack of brand new robes that looked very attractive, so I went over to look. There was a lot of action there, and I had to wedge my way in towards the rack. The area was a mess, with lots of merchandise already strewn around the floor. It was a struggle, but I finally found a robe that I liked, grabbed it, and took a look at the price tag. It seemed like a fair price, so I decided to buy it and started off to find the cashier.

As I was walking away, I noticed for the first time that there was a big sign over the robes rack that said, "EVERYTHING ON THIS RACK 25% OFF." "Wow," I thought, "isn't that great." I went over to pay for it and saw that there were perhaps fifty people on line waiting to pay at the cash register. This didn't look too promising. "If I get at the end of that line," I thought, "it will be an hour before I can pay for this thing. That's ridiculous."

I put the robe back on the rack and I left.

As I was walking out of the store, I passed the uncrowded watch counter, quickly picked up a fun watch, paid for it, and called it a day.

I thought about what was going on in that department, the number of robes they were selling, and the fact that they were giving back 25% of the regular sales price to consumers who didn't expect it, didn't come in for that promotion and would have been there anyway because they needed a Mother's Day gift. As far as I was concerned, they were giving away their profits.

Soon after this experience, the president of that store came to the showroom. I told him my Mother's Day story. I said, "I know it's none of my business, but how much volume do you do in that robe department the day before Mother's Day? How much do you do totally in all of your stores? You must do at least like $1,000,000."

He replied, "It's probably a lot more than that, but let's just say it's $1,000,000."

"If you gave away 25% of that in promotions, you might have taken $250,000 out of the gross margin for the day that you otherwise could have gotten. There's no question in my mind that those same customers would have bought those robes. It was Mother's Day! Just think of what you could have done with that $250,000! You could have had more salespeople on the floor to help people, to put the merchandise back on the racks, to keep the department neat. You could have had more cashiers at the checkout counter so there wouldn't be fifty people waiting on line for an hour. You could have taken those same dollars that you just gave away for no reason and made the whole shopping experience better for the consumer."

My friend was furious. He shook his head and said, "Do me a favor, Jerry. You run your business and let me run mine."

And he stomped out of my office.

Over time, the cost of such sales became uncontrollable, and the hit that the retailers took on their profits was a disaster for them. So what did they do? They came right back to the manufacturers that they were buying from to make the case that they should be given some cash back. They would say, "We can't sell your merchandise at full price. Here's a list of the markdowns we had to take. Now we need your help, or we'll have to reconsider how much business we can do with you in the future."

Of course, the real problem was this new "creative" use of price changes. Retailers had trained consumers to shop the sale – to wait until one of these very regular, very frequent promotions took place. Why pay full price? Consumers never had to wait too long to find the items they needed offered at a reduced price.

When all this first started, we tried to stand tall as a company. We told the retailers, "You cannot include Liz Claiborne in these sales. We want our merchandise selling at regular price. We're giving the consumer good value, she certainly seems willing to pay for it, and we want to continue that way. If you are going to carry Liz Claiborne, keep it at regular price until you have your end-of-season sales. Otherwise, don't buy our merchandise."

Our stance worked for a time, but now our merchandise was on the floor at regular price, while our competitors' was being sold at a discount. The consumer would see this and think, "I'd really rather have the Liz jacket, but it's $150, and right over there I can buy a similar jacket from Jones New York that was $150 and is now on sale now for $110." A percentage of our customers started saying, "I'll buy the jacket for $110. Forty bucks is forty bucks."

At some point we had to give in, or we would be at a tremendous disadvantage with the consumer. The trend was just too strong to fight.

It was all so easy. Markdown rates zoomed out of control and profits started to be affected and, still, the practice not only continued, but mushroomed.

A new term was invented to describe this activity: "POS" – point of sale markdowns.

The situation has not gotten any better. I remember Macy's used to have a great big "one day sale" on Wednesday, and they would do it two or three times a year. Then they started doing them more often. Then they would extend it by advertising the sale in Tuesday's newspaper and inviting customers to "preview" the Wednesday sale on Tuesday. So now it's a two day sale. And now they are having these sales virtually every single week. Same goes for Memorial Day sales, which now start mid week the week *before* Memorial Day, and so forth.

These days, there are certain department stores where virtually every apparel rack has a markdown sign on top. Consumers today have to question what the real price is. The one that is printed on the ticket has no meaning. And still, retailers persist. I have spoken to any number of store presidents about the problem. They shrug their shoulders, and say, "Jerry, this is the new reality of doing business."

Well, doing business this way destroyed retailing as we knew it, and it has never recovered.

It's not all to the consumer's benefit, either. In trying to cope with this sales environment, some retailers turned to "creative" pricing strategies. The so called "40% off" price in reality represents the price the retailer actually wants for the item. Shoppers now need to be much more aware that the high initial ticket price they see on the garment may be artificial and designed to be marked down. Consumers need to be vigorous in their understanding of the real worth of any purchase.

All of this caused tremendous problems at Liz Claiborne. We were constantly trying to come up with new and better ways of selling to consumers. So much of what we tried to do, including new marketing concepts, more attractive fixtures, providing salespeople with more product information, was overwhelmed by the constant sales in the stores. It led to one of the biggest disappointments of my career – the failure of our freestanding Liz Claiborne stores.

Let me back up a bit:

There was a desire on our part to control not only the design and manufacture of the merchandise, but also the approach to the consumer – the way in which the merchandise is shown and marketed at the retail level. The obvious way to do this was to break out of the department store model and build our own Liz Claiborne stores where we would compete with companies like Ann Taylor and Talbots.

With our Liz Claiborne departments in the department stores, essentially we were running a store within a store. We were doing vertical retailing like any specialty store. So why not take the next step and open up our own freestanding stores around the country? We would lessen our dependency on the department stores, and we would have better control of our future.

Our attempt to develop our own stores was another rule breaker. We were trying something different. No other apparel manufacturer with our tremendous level of department store business and widespread distribution had ever done this. Ralph Lauren's products, as an example, were in far more limited distribution and he was able to make a go of his stand-alone shops.

Our logic included the fact that many customers were much more comfortable shopping in specialty stores. The typical mall already had dozens of them, so why shouldn't we join in and appeal directly to those consumers shopping in those malls?

One mall operator I knew and liked was Alfred Taubman. He was CEO of the Taubman company and while not the largest mall operator, I always felt he was the most innovative and classiest. I met with Al, told him about our decision to open our own stores, and between us we decided that the Twelve Oaks Mall in suburban Detroit would be an ideal first location for a store.

We opened our first Liz Claiborne store in the spring of 1988. It was very close to one belonging to our second largest retail customer at the time, the J. L. Hudson Company. We spoke to their executives, told them we were going to open the store, and they reluctantly accepted the news. We were convinced that the new store would not affect their business, and as it turned out, it didn't. There were plenty of customers for both specialty stores and department stores.

Our experience in Twelve Oaks was a good one and as a result we opened several more stores to continue the concept test. We placed them in appropriate malls around the country and used them as a learning experience for new merchandise and new merchandising ideas.

At one point a space in midtown Manhattan became available. We signed a lease and opened a showcase store on 5th Avenue and 53rd Street. We wanted it to be an international tourist destination, with people from all over country and the world visiting us and seeing Liz Claiborne merchandise shown under the best of circumstances.

We wanted this flagship store to be special and a little different. As a glass collector, I had become friendly with Dale Chihuly, perhaps the most important glass artist in the country. Many people call him the Louis Comfort Tiffany of the 20th century. I suggested to Dale that it might be possible to install a major Chihuly exhibit so that he would be permanently represented on Fifth Avenue in New York. He loved the idea and created an amazing group of glass sculptures that covered one of the walls of the store. It became an instant landmark.

We felt that we were far enough away from our good customers, the retail department stores in town: Macy's was way down on 34th Street, and Bloomingdale's across town at 59th and Third Avenue.

Soon however, the facts of life started to sink in.

We had a beautiful dress department in that store. One day a customer came in, bought a dress that she needed for an evening out, and paid the $200 retail price. Our salespeople took very good care of her, and she actually went up to the manager after she made the purchase and told him how pleased she was with the service and what a pleasant experience it was.

The next day, this same customer came back to return the dress! She was embarrassed and very apologetic. She had been in Macy's, and they were selling our dress – the same Liz Claiborne dress – at 40% off. That was a difference of $80 to our customer. She told our people, "If it were just a few dollars, I wouldn't bring it back, but $80 is a lot of money. I'm sorry, I have to return it."

This incident was a very clear warning regarding the challenge of competing against the sales mentality of the department stores. Since the heart of our business was selling merchandise – much the same as the merchandise we were selling in our own stores – to department stores with branches in every single important mall in America, there was no place for us to hide. Where could we put our stores where we wouldn't be competing against sale after sale and promotion after promotion? The answer was *nowhere*.

Mayor Guiliani- DaleChihuly and others at 5th Avenue Store Opening.

We stuck with it for a while and opened a number of new stores. But the promotional posture of the department stores made it impossible for us to keep up with their pricing and still afford the level of superior service and store ambience that we wanted to provide our customers with. We could see that other specialty retailers had a big advantage over us with their different business model – consumers would not be able to find their merchandise in the department stores at all, let alone at discounted prices. They, unlike Liz Claiborne, were in the fortunate position of not having to compete with the big stores on price.

Eventually, sometime after I left the company, the Liz Claiborne retail operation was shut down. I know in my heart that if we had started these stores early, before we became so wedded to selling to the department stores, we would have succeeded.

When we realized the difficulty of trying to have our own Liz Claiborne retail stores, we thought maybe we could open up another kind of independent retail chain under another name not associated with Liz and take advantage of our manufacturing capability and our merchandising strengths. Two major factors moved us in this direction:

The Fifth Avenue Store.

Jerome A. Chazen

Not surprisingly, we had began to see that more and more of our customers were becoming very price conscious, like the lady who returned the dress. How could they help it, living in this environment of constant sales and promotions?

The second factor was our growing concern about having the department stores as a long term customer. We didn't see much that was good happening in their world. We disagreed with many of their practices. The department store chains were having a very difficult time, and some were going into bankruptcy. It became more and more apparent that we needed to be in control of our destiny as much as we possibly could.

We started a company that would sell separates, as we were doing at Liz, only at lower prices. Here again, I would say the board reluctantly went along with the strategy, but we got the business started. We wanted the new company and its label to be different from Liz in the eyes of the consumer, so we named it First Issue, and we went out and hired an entirely new group of people to staff it. We used almost nobody from the Liz Claiborne organization except for some employees who helped in the production area. The design and merchandising staffs were different, and so of course, were the new people we hired as sales staff for the stores.

We tried to make it a totally autonomous operation that wouldn't interfere with the work at Liz. But it really didn't turn out that way. Running two companies was much more complicated than that. We found that it was very expensive operating two companies at the same time, and a lot of expenses at Liz became part of the cost structure of the new company. This prevented us from being as competitive with the other retail chains as I think we should have been. Plus we may have had the wrong leadership in place at First Issue.

At any rate we gave it a big try. We eventually opened forty or fifty stores and then ended up throwing in the towel in 1995. So there we were. It didn't work. It turned out to be a big mistake.

Sometimes you break the rules, and sometimes the rules break you.

The markdown situation, this era of constant promotions, not only hurt us in our attempt to operate our own stores, but it also became one of a number of factors in the collapse of many department stores during the late 1980s and early 1990s, a situation that had a horrible effect on our industry.

152

The 1980s was the decade of junk bonds, corporate raiders, and leveraged buyouts. Money was plentiful – but at a very high price – for risk happy businesspeople who wanted to take over companies. The idea was to finance a corporate takeover – often "hostile," meaning the company's management was opposed to the takeover – by using huge sums of borrowed money to purchase controlling interest in a company's stock. The purchased company would then be saddled with paying off the debt used in the takeover and would have to divert millions of dollars of revenue to the bond holders, money that would normally be put back into the business to keep it operating effectively and growing. These kinds of deals are perhaps epitomized by the infamous debt-financed buyout of RJR Nabisco by Kohlberg Kravis Roberts in 1988.

The department stores were not immune to these highly-leveraged financial shenanigans, and it was a constant worry of their management that they would catch the eye of a corporate raider. Macy's was our largest customer, so of course anything that happened to them was of considerable concern to Liz Claiborne.

Ed Finkelstein, the CEO of Macy's, was one executive who felt his store was ripe for a hostile takeover. In order to keep his company out of the hands of the raiders, in 1986 he engineered a buyout in which company executives participated. Much of the financing was done with junk bonds, which burdened the company with a mountain of dept. But the result was that Ed and his colleagues became the owners of Macy's.

Macy's under Ed Finkelstein had quite a run. He expanded the business far and wide across the country, turning Macy's into a vital national retail organization. But Ed himself was not a financial expert nor, I think, did he consider himself one. He was a merchant, though, who believed that he could run a better department store than his competitors could.

Attempts to expand operations, such as Macy's move to create concept stores around some of their private label brands (Charter Club, Aeropostale, and others), were ill-considered. Executives were not paying enough attention to the financial implications of their expansion plans at a time when consumers were beginning to slow down their buying, while the stores desperately tried to lure them back with their markdown promotion approach. The traditional approach to full-price retailing was dead.

The Macy's people, when times were good, perhaps took their retail prowess a bit too much for granted. I remember a discussion I had in Art Reiner's office. Art was the president of Macy's New York, working directly under Ed Finkelstein. The company had just announced that they were going to open a store in Texas. I asked Art how carefully they had considered this move to Texas: what sort of studies they had done? What consumer demographics they had discovered? What about the competition – in Dallas in particular?

Art's answer was astonishing. "We flew down to Texas. We took a look at Sanger Brothers, and we said, 'We can teach these guys how to do business.' That was enough for us."

So there was some arrogance on the part of Macy's executives, believing they didn't make mistakes, that they could do it better than anyone else. To me, this attitude was just another illustration of an industry out of control.

One of the people Ed had been worried about was Robert Campeau, an upstart entrepreneur from Canada. In 1986 Campeau, backed by junk bond financing, gained control of Allied Stores, which owned many department stores, including Jordan Marsh, Garfinkels, and Brooks Brothers .

Our second largest customer Federated Department Stores, was joining the fray. In many ways Federated was the classiest and most historically important group of stores in the country, even going back into the 19th century. Famous stores in the Federated family included Bloomingdale's and Abraham and Strauss. Federated had a sterling reputation among vendors and consumers and often operated the most important store in any city in which they were located.

Then Campeau stepped in. He went after Federated. With the help of some unbelievably naïve financial institutions, more money was made available to this gentleman. Borrowing billions, he was able to take over the Federated organization in 1988. In doing so, he piled up the company with debt – a financial burden that would eventually prove fatal to this once great institution.

We were at the time the single largest supplier to Federated and were less than thrilled by this turn of events. Allen Questrom, who was running the company, called me and told me that Mr. Campeau wanted to visit Liz Claiborne so that he could make us feel more comfortable about his new role at Federated. He walked into our offices with an entourage. There must have been eight or ten Federated executives with him.

I asked Mr. Campeau if he wanted to talk, look at product, or hear about our company. All he really seemed interested in was holding forth – talking at us about how Federated was going to control the retail world. Frankly I wasn't impressed. In fact, I was concerned. From everything that I had read about the man, I knew he had no retail background. As I looked around the room at some of his executives, I wondered about the future of Federated and how their jobs would be affected by the new ownership.

In spite of my misgivings, our relationship with Federated continued. What choice did we have? The financial side of doing business with them became very risky, as they had to devote so much of their cash flow to paying off the debt Campeau incurred to buy the company.

Jim Zimmerman, president and CFO of Federated at the time, to his credit tried to keep the company alive by working with the vendors and massaging their financial terms, all in an effort to keep us shipping them goods to sell.

We were so concerned about their ongoing ability to pay us that we sent one of our accounting people to Federated's corporate headquarters in Cincinnati to wait for our checks to be issued and rush them to the bank for deposit. We didn't want to take any chances that Federated would run out of money.

The other side of Campeau's battle for Federated is what it did to Macy's. When Federated was in play as a result of Campeau's attempts to take it over, Macy's management got into the mix and tried to win Federated for itself. They lost out, but did manage to buy two California-based retail chains in the Federated family that Campeau was willing to part with. Macy's ended up spending $1.1 billion for Bullock's and I. Magnin, a high fashion specialty store. The transaction added additional debt to Macy's already clouded financial picture.

Burdened with all this crushing debt, by end of 1988, Macy's and Federated were posting losses in the millions of dollars. At the same time, consumers were starting to shift their buying patterns away from the traditional department stores and toward specialty stores, outlet stores, and the big box discounters.

The department stores were running out of money as they tried to meet their debt obligations and cut expenses elsewhere. They began to do everything "on the cheap," which meant the complete dissolution of many of the important elements that made the department store special: the loss of quality people at every level, in-store display managers, operations people, salespeople on the floor. One very significant result was a deterioration of the shopping experience for the consumer.

It was a tough time for the entire apparel industry, but Liz kept growing. We were in the right place at the right time, catering to women's clothing needs as they entered into the workforce in droves. They needed clothes to go to work in, and we had what they wanted and needed. The bad news though, was that we were so dependent on the department stores, and our continued success was tied to a considerable degree to their fate.

In January, 1990, Federated sought bankruptcy protection. At the time it was the largest retail bankruptcy in history.

Macy's, our single largest customer, was also in trouble, and we knew it. We were afraid to ship them merchandise, worried that we would never be paid. At one point we thought seriously about cutting them off, and that's when I got a call from Ed Finkelstein. It was a Friday in January, 1992.

"Jerry," Ed said, "Liz is our most important supplier. The rest of the marketplace is very aware of how you are treating us, whether you believe we are viable or not. If you stop shipping, everyone will stop. I'm begging you, please continue to ship."

Ed's pleas did not fall on deaf ears. Even though they owed us around $20 million, we discussed the issue amongst ourselves and decided to ship them $50,000 worth of merchandise that Friday afternoon. They declared bankruptcy the following Monday, January 27, 1992.

As I think back over those tumultuous years, it seems amazing to me that we were able to continue to function with our two largest customers on the ropes. We took a big hit with the bankruptcies, and if we were any other kind of company, it could have put us out of business. Thankfully we were in terrific financial shape, and we could take it, in spite of our dependence on the department stores for sales.

Chapter 8

Growth and Expansion Around the World

We so dominated the department stores with our product that, as we looked strategically at where our growth would come from next, one of the things we talked about was whether our Liz Claiborne consumer – our Lizzy -- existed outside of the United States. It seemed to us that she did.

At this point in the company's development we were well into our understanding of women returning to the workforce and the ways we could serve them. The same movement was taking place outside the United States, but somewhat more slowly.

The European economies were more deeply affected by World War II than was the US. The damage to the infrastructure, the loss of life, and all the horrors of war that Europe experienced took a lot of time to get over compared to the situation in the US. There was no question that women there were going to work, and we saw a chance to provide them with the kind of clothing that their counterparts in the US were wearing.

But first we first set our sights on Canada – it seemed the most obvious way to extend our reach outside of the continental United States. We knew that 90% of the Canadian population (which was about 10% the size of the US) lived within 100 miles of the US-Canadian border. Canadians watch American TV. They see American movies. They vacation in the US, and many were already buying Liz Claiborne merchandise during their visits.

So we felt there were plenty of Lizzies up there, and some of them were already our consumer.

The easiest way for us to get started was to do in Canada exactly what we were doing in the United States: sell the department stores. We opened an office in Toronto and hired Canadians to staff it. We never had a showroom in Canada, though. Our employees were there to service the stores after they received their merchandise. Perhaps it seemed arrogant, but we suggested that Canadian store buyers come to New York to see the line – just as every US buyer did. In fact, many of our US customers had to travel greater distances to see us than the Canadians did. None of the retailers objected to these trips, and our sales staff in New York was quite capable of working with them.

The Canadian retail scene had many fewer players than the States. All of the department store executives were very familiar with Liz Claiborne, as they shopped the American stores on a regular basis, and many belonged to the same international buying offices. The Hudson Bay Company, which I always felt was very similar to Macy's, was the oldest department store in North America. Their original stores in the northern part of the country began as fur trading posts, and many of them still existed. We were very comfortable developing a business plan and taking all of the marketing tools that we were using in the States and applying them to "The Bay," as they liked to be called.

The slightly higher end department store was Eaton's, and it had been successful in Canada for many years. We equated it to Bloomingdale's and treated it accordingly. Here too, they were very receptive to our ideas and like "The Bay, instead of starting real small and allowing business to build naturally, they were interested in doing maximum volume as fast as they could. We loved it.

Canada even had a large specialty store operation comparable to Saks and Neiman's called Holt Renfrew. We immediately became a significant volume player with this store even though we were at the low end of their price structure. As a matter of fact, when we started Dana Buchman, Holt Renfrew became one of our largest customers.

Our move into Canada was a huge success.

We learned a lot about selling in a foreign country. We faced many logistical problems having to do with duties and import-export regulations that we had to figure out. On the other hand, Canada was playing catch up with their American cousins and wanted to work with us – so in many ways it was as if we were just adding some new domestic accounts.

These Canadian companies were buying exactly the same product that we were making for the American market – there were no differences at all. And it turned out that the success of our lines in that country was equal to the success that we had in the US.

We began our operations in Canada in 1988. In the following year we expanded both our product offerings and our facilities and we reached $27.1 million in sales. In 1990, sales grew to above $40 million.

Canada was so easy that it didn't really prepare us for the arduous journey across the ocean once we decided to conquer Europe. That journey began with the United Kingdom. We stated in our 1989 annual report that we anticipated beginning our first shipments there in early 1991, and that we were "excited about the prospects."

It turned out that things were not quite so easy in the UK.

We were the first American company to go to Europe and try to become a traditional wholesaler selling to department stores primarily. It soon became obvious to us that Liz Claiborne, as important as it was in both the US and now Canada, was almost completely unknown as a brand – and Liz herself as a designer – in Great Britain. We were going to have to start from scratch, prove our product all over again and try to build a business. On the positive side, we thought that our merchandise was appropriate and that we wouldn't have to make any significant changes to either design or color. And we felt that our prices would also be competitive.

It's not as though England and Europe were just waiting for us to show up. The UK had its own apparel industry that was extremely important in their domestic market. Britain was also home to many of the continental designer brands and, in our price category, many firms from Germany. The ability of the European countries to deal with one another was much simpler, without the difficulties we had with duties and quotas. The various firms that we would be competing with in the UK had been doing business throughout Europe for decades.

In some ways I think that we were overconfident. We had been so successful at home in pleasing our consumer that it seemed like all we had to do was expose our merchandise to the English people and they would respond as positively as the Americans and Canadians had done.

We tried to use the same marketing and selling tools in the UK that were successful for us in the States and in Canada. We opened an office and showroom in London, contacted the various store buyers, and invited them to come and see our line. The buyers, for the most part, had at least heard of Liz Claiborne, and many of the larger store buyers did travel to the US at least occasionally. So people came and looked. We of course thought of the major department stores first and talked to Harrods, Selfridges, Harvey Nichols and several other major players in London.

Everyone was polite and for the most part appreciative but not overwhelmed by what they saw. The strength of our firm had never been avant-garde or shocking design – we made nice, tasteful garments that were perfect for a certain woman's lifestyle needs. What wowed our retailers at home was the performance of the line, and we tried to get that idea across to our English friends.

Our business model, so successful in the US, was unknown in the UK. Wholesalers there operated in the same way that the US wholesale industry did when we started our company in 1976. We were faced with the same situation that we had coped with successfully in the States of putting all of the merchandise into production before we had any orders from stores.

Could we change the way business was being done in the UK? It proved to be quite a challenge.

The concept of selling into our ownership was a struggle with every buyer we met. They didn't understand why they couldn't buy our merchandise the same way they did with every other wholesaler. We created a UK package and did our best to sell into our ownership. We were breaking the rules all over again, this time in a foreign country, and in almost every case we did succeed in getting the stores to try the merchandise.

Unfortunately, we began to encounter delivery problems on the orders we received. In the States we were able to do a reasonably accurate forecast of what the retailers would buy, and we also had the added advantage of our own department and dollar amounts that would almost guarantee each season. Now it was all a guessing game, and we had to respond as best we could after the orders were placed. As a result, many of the stores became unhappy with our performance in that area. It was just one more stumbling block to our success.

There were also logistical problems that we had to solve. All of our merchandise was made in Asia. We had to ship to a warehouse facility in Europe and then ship to the stores. There were all kinds of new and unfamiliar regulations what we had to cope with, but we did make that part of it work.

While we were facing a great many problems, still, no one at Liz wanted to surrender. We felt we could be successful, and so we did what we could to shore up Great Britain. We managed to build up a nice business with a variety of department stores in London and in many of the larger British cities.

Then we moved on to the continent, where geographic realities hit us almost immediately. France and Italy were so protective of their own apparel industries that not only was there no welcome mat put out for us, but people we spoke with in both countries told us we would just be wasting our time.

The key to Europe, we learned, was Germany. It had the largest population and, having recovered from the devastation of World War II, had an affluent consumer base. One of my friends in the US told me that I should go to Frankfurt and check out the Apparel Trade Fair held there. Retailers from all over Europe would be attending to examine and buy merchandise from all the European manufacturers. The Fair was the main venue for independent specialty stores to examine upcoming lines and place orders for goods they would be selling in the future. This was a very different way of doing business than in the States, where buyers would come to the manufacturers' showrooms to see the product.

When I walked into the trade fair headquarters, I completely was blown away by the size and volume of manufacturers exhibiting their products and store buyers walking the halls. There was nothing like it in America.

A meeting at the show had been arranged for me with Klaus Steilmann, who was the CEO of one of the largest apparel companies in Germany. I found my way to the Steilmann selling area. It was a beehive of activity with merchandise being shown, lots of salespeople, and what seemed like dozens of retailers milling about or meeting with the salespeople.

I tried to get a moment with Herr Steilmann, telling him that I was from Liz Claiborne and that a mutual acquaintance had suggested that we meet. Well, he was a very, very busy man, running around from retailer to retailer, talking, selling – doing business. In fact he seemed to be the ace salesman of the company.

When I got his attention, I quickly said, "I would just like to spend a few minutes with you. I'll wait until you have time."

He replied in excellent English, "It will be awhile, but I'll talk to you."

I finally did get my moment with him. Before I could say a word or even utter a pleasantry, he began, "I know all about your company."

"Oh?"

"You're doing a very good job in America."

I smiled at that, thinking we were about to launch into a nice, cordial conversation. I replied, "Thank you very much!"

His next words were not so cordial. "Stay there. Stay in America. We don't need you in Germany. We have enough companies, enough resources, and we don't need anybody from America telling us what kind of clothes we're supposed to wear."

What could I say? I thanked him very much for his welcoming speech and left.

We had some decisions to make. We went back and reassessed the whole situation in Germany, Holland, Belgium and Scandinavia. Here was another eye-opener for us: There were virtually no malls in Europe. Instead, there were lots of towns and cities close to one another each with its own downtown. The department store share of the apparel market was minimal. The retail clothing business was dominated by small independent specialty stores with very few chains. So not only did we have all these domestic suppliers to compete with, but the landscape was completely different from the one in the US, where we had been so successful.

We knew that we were so department store oriented there was no way we could change the character of our company to do business with the small independent retailers. But we felt that if we could get the major dept stores to do business with us, it might bring us some significant results.

One advantage we did have was that the European department stores had relationships with the department stores in the United States. There were many international meetings and contacts between them since American department stores had always purchased European products. (Unlike the Europeans who rarely bought American products.) So we thought we could at least get into the front door.

We did manage to sell major department stores throughout the European continent. What was shocking to us was how small the volumes were, a function of the small size of many of the cities in these countries.

We also learned quite a bit about legal issues in Europe. In every one of the countries, there were national laws that set forth what days and hours retailers could be open. No stores could open on Sunday. Stores closed by 2PM on Saturday. There were evening hours only one night a week. Then I learned that not only were the hours a matter of law, but so were some of the ways they did business. Sales could only be run twice a year, in January and July. The one-day sales, holiday promotions, and all the other excuses for a sale that the US stores used were against the law in Europe. I found that hard to believe until one day I was in Brussels talking to the general merchandise manager of one of the department stores when he got a phone call: there was a warrant out for the arrest of the store president for advertising a sale at an improper time. I had to smile when I thought about what these restrictions would do to the American retailers, forcing them to sell much of their merchandise at regular price.

Hiring practices also were very difficult and different from what we were used to. In Europe we were operating in a socialist environment, and once the employee was on the books, it was almost impossible to let him or her go. We learned to live with these and other laws and depended on the sales of our merchandise to pay for all of the problems we encountered.

The interaction between our employees in the States and those throughout Europe was also not as effective as it could be. I think that many of the people in our US offices, instead of welcoming the international business, thought of it as a nuisance and a distraction from the main event. In those years, video conferencing was just beginning, but we latched onto it, hoping that it would bring our people closer together. It helped a little, but nothing can ever replace the day-to-day, face-to-face relationships.

In other ways Europe was a good learning experience that helped us develop better ways to run the company. We had to be nimble and move quickly to surmount logistical problems that surfaced on an almost daily basis. Or original warehouse was located in England, which worked for the UK but was difficult for Europe. So we relocated to a beautiful warehouse facility in Holland.

We even experimented with setting up Liz departments as concessions in some of the department stores. We operated the departments totally, as if they were our own, paying rent as a percentage of sales to the store itself.

To some degree, our international sales over the years are a reflection of all these tough issues we had to face. In 1991, we wrote in the annual report that our global market efforts had just begun. International sales that year were $84 million. The company's total net sales were $2 billion, so international represented about 4% of sales.

By the end of 1992, we were seeing growth. We were established in Canada and were beginning to sell in Western Europe, the Pacific Rim, the Caribbean, and Latin America. International total net sales were $101.8 million. That year, total Liz Claiborne net sales were $2.1 billion, so international represented less than 5% of our business. By 1995, our international sales had reached $138 million.

In spite of all the obstacles and unfamiliar ways of doing business, we kept trying. But the international sales we did achieve were never more than a small percentage of our company's total sales and not very significant to us. Wall Street didn't see it as very important either.

Even though business overseas turned out not to be a big deal for us, it was significant in terms of the European markets themselves and actually made us one of the bigger apparel companies on the continent at that time. And our achievements over there probably represented the largest penetration of these markets by any American clothing firm.

Chapter 9

Last Days at Liz

When the four partners started Liz Claiborne, none of us were kids. As I mentioned earlier in the book, Art, Liz, and myself were in our late 40s, and Leonard was over 50. We had all spent our whole careers working for other people, and we had opinions about our bosses and the ways they ran their businesses. Unlike the way some of our former bosses operated, we felt strongly that our employees deserved to be treated as well as possible. We never wanted the success of the company to benefit just the owners – we wanted to share the rewards. We never took outrageous salaries even when things were going very well. Once we became a public company and had the ability to issue options, none of the founders ever took any. Frankly, our stock ownership alone had made each us wealthy beyond our dreams, and that was enough. With that kind of background, corporate governance was very much a part of our DNA.

One of our directors, Lou Lowenstein, looked at corporate governance practices throughout the country. One of the issues that came up in his research was nepotism. We wanted to address that and make sure it didn't exist in the company – and it didn't. In my case, I never asked any of my three kids to become involved in the business. They each had their own career path, and any successes they achieved were due to their own efforts.

Another big issue was retirement. We established 70 as the age beyond which no executive should remain with the company. At the time, it seemed like a very good rule. We gave executives five years more than the traditional social security retirement age of 65, and we had no problem getting it into our corporate by-laws.

Unfortunately, the rule wasn't so good for me, as age 70 just seemed to zoom up out of nowhere. Leonard, Liz, and Art had all retired years before. I was the last of the founders, but I wanted to play by the rules we had established and leave the company when it was time. As the months went on, the board became antsy about finding my successor, as it didn't seem that any of our current employees could take over the company.

I agreed with the board's assessment. Jay Margolis, who was our merchandizing head, had a good feel for fashion. He was good with product, but I felt he did not have the knowledge and experience to run such a big and complex organization. Harvey Falk, our President, had risen from CFO to being in charge of all production. He wasn't a "merchant" in the sense of having much experience marketing to the retailers or dealing with the consumer.

As far as I could see or the board could see, there was no one else in house to consider. That meant we had to go outside. We wanted somebody who had it all – who was a merchant, understood fashion, and still had the business skills to run what had become a multi-billion dollar company doing business all over the world.

It was a tough and demanding job, and we couldn't even see anybody in any of the other apparel companies who might fit our needs. We were just so large – a $2 billion company. The typical apparel company at the time was doing $50 or $60 million. They were babies. We were huge. We had thousands of employees. We needed somebody with major business and management background to step into a company that size, and we felt we just couldn't take a chance with somebody who had only run one of these tiny companies in our industry, no matter how successful they were.

At one point I thought it might make sense to bring in a fashion retailer who was running one of the big department store chains. Most of the important retailers had many stores and thousands of employees. An executive from one of these companies, even though he might not be involved in manufacturing, would understand fashion, the consumer market, and the industry in general.

One man who I thought would be right for Liz Claiborne was Burt Tansky, who had just been offered the presidency of Neiman Marcus. We were friendly and talked about the job, but his response was, in so many words, "Your company is terrific. But, frankly, I know how to run Neiman Marcus. I'm not sure I know how to run Liz Claiborne."

We brought in a search firm to help us, and we considered all kinds of people. I had one favorite, a man I liked very much by the name of Roger Farah. He would have been my first choice. Roger had gone up the ladder at Saks Fifth Ave and had made an interesting move to become the CEO of the F. W. Woolworth Company. Everyone thinks of Woolworth's as a "five and dime," but at the time it was one of the largest retail empires in the world. Subsequently, Roger left that job and became president of the Ralph Lauren Company where he has done an outstanding job creating what many people feel is the best apparel company in the world.

At any rate, an attractive candidate named Paul Charron came in to talk to us. Paul was ex-Navy, a graduate of Notre Dame, Harvard Business school, plus he was involved in consumer products. He had worked for Proctor & Gamble where he was head of one of their divisions, and he was currently a key executive at VF, a huge company that was one of our competitors in denim apparel. VF owned Lee Jeans and Wrangler Jeans and many other businesses, and they were bigger than Liz. They owned some lingerie companies and Paul was in charge of that group. In a sense he was the man who managed the operation, watched the numbers, but really didn't touch the product.

But at least, we thought, he had a taste of what the fashion business was all about, and he was a nice guy. We spent time together, he liked our company, and he came to believe that he could do the job. The board agreed, and we brought him into Liz Claiborne to be my successor a full year before my retirement was going to become official. The idea was that we would have the opportunity to work together before I rode off into the sunset.

In my year with Paul, I tried to recreate him in my image. But it really didn't work. In many ways he was more organized financially, more buttoned up in strategy meetings, but I just couldn't get him involved in the products we were creating. He didn't respond to the apparel and other merchandise and didn't seem to like attending the meetings where they were discussed. He shared with me that he didn't really have a feel for women's apparel. He also didn't enjoy being in the showroom and interfacing with buyers, although he was articulate and well spoken and could handle himself with store presidents. He couldn't really get into the trenches of our business.

Since I felt so strongly that product was the key to the success of our company, I was convinced that the man at the top had to have passion for all the things we created and merchandized season after season. Paul and I discussed this, and I told him that we needed a partner for him who had that passion, and that the two of them together could be a dynamic team. I equated this to the department store field where the traditional structure at the top was a president and a chairman, one of whom was responsible for the product in the stores and the other for all of the operations. Paul didn't disagree. Neither did the board when I explained the situation to them.

I told the board that I was so concerned and felt so strongly about this issue that I wasn't going to leave until we found somebody to take on the product role. It wasn't a threat as much as a signal that we had a serious problem here.

We did a search and brought in Denise Seegal. Denise had quite an extensive background in the fashion industry. She was very much a garment person. I had run into Denise from time to time over the years and felt that she certainly had the background to watch over the fashion end of the company. I was somewhat concerned as to whether she would have the toughness to be Paul's match and to carry on as his equal in the organization.

When we decided to hire her, Denise and I sat down and had a real heart to heart. I told her how important it was for her to be strong and to stand up for the Liz Claiborne fashion product. She understood and said, "I've dealt with businessmen like Paul before and feel very confident that I can work with him. I really want this job, and I know I can do it."

So we brought her in as President, and gave her a two year contract. With Denise in place, I felt that it was time for me to go. My official turnover of the reins took place at the annual meeting in May, 1996. I made a little speech and handed the gavel to Paul.

On my last day in the office, I met with Paul, wished him well and told him I was confident I was leaving the company in good hands. I added as a reminder, "I'm leaving you the best apparel company in the country and

$400 million in cash." I thought that was a pretty good goodbye gift from me to the company and to my successor. When I walked out the door, I felt that the foundation was in place for Liz Claiborne to go on, hopefully forever.

It was difficult saying goodbye to the people in the company – people I had worked with for all those wonderful years, some from the very beginning. But as far as Liz Claiborne Inc, was concerned, I had done my job, done it well, and was leaving the business in great shape.

I have to say that I was ready to go. Having worked with Paul over that year, I had handed over more and more of my responsibilities to him and in the process separated gradually from the company. It didn't happen overnight – it wasn't as though I ran the business until the last possible second, went to bed, and woke up the next morning without a job. I had gotten used to the idea of not being there, so it wasn't at all a wrenching experience. Plus, Simona and I had talked about it a lot. I was fully prepared to no longer be Chairman of Liz Claiborne.

I didn't even want to use the term "retired" in the description of my departure from the company, because I felt like what I was really doing was starting a new career – even though I wasn't exactly sure what that career would be. What I did know was that I needed to be in an office every day working on something that I would enjoy and that would keep me engaged. I also knew that whatever I did would not be in the fashion world. I was determined that there would be life after Liz Claiborne.

People constantly ask me what I think about what's happened to the company in the time since I left. All I'll say is that it's obvious the years have not been kind to Liz Claiborne. The company has changed dramatically and, unfortunately, not for the better. It's easy to sit out on the sidelines and criticize, so I'm not going to do that. Many difficult problems arose, and perhaps they weren't handled as well as they could have been. But again, sitting here and judging is a lot easier than being in the hot seat dealing with the tough issues day in and day out and trying to come up with the best solutions.

The truth is that I don't dwell on the company and its fate. In fact, I believe that one of the reasons for my writing this book is to give me a chance to think about it once again and bring back and preserve my memories of the glory days at Liz.

Epilogue

My Life after Liz Claiborne

Now I am out of Liz Claiborne. I left the company in 1996 and opened up my own office. As I am writing this book, I'm still in the same space. I share the office suite with my son David and my son-in-law Sid Banon. They were partners in a company headquartered in Long Island City, and when I first started talking about setting up an office, they asked if I couldn't put some space in it for them. That way, they could have a New York presence for their business. I was more than pleased to do it. The more the merrier, I figured.

The office has grown with David, Sid, and my valued executive assistant, Mona Mayer, who was with me at Liz for ten years before my departure. We hired a receptionist, Theresa Murtagh, and Sid brought in Eric Chan, one of his accounting people from the Long Island City office. David and Sid pay for their portion of the rent, and it feels like a good business arrangement for everybody.

The office is in the General Motors building facing Central Park. There are beautiful views of the park and other parts of New York from our windows. My personal office was built to be a virtual duplicate of my office at Liz. As a matter of fact, Liz allowed me to take all of my furniture with me. Simona felt strongly about making the space as attractive as possible, so I would be pleased to go to work every day. It was a very good idea and has worked well.

President George Rupp & Dean Meyer Feldberg -- Columbia University.

I was in my new office, but I didn't have my new business yet. I had a strong desire to invest in new companies and use my business skills to help them get started and hopefully prosper. We set up a company called Chazen Capital Partners, and Sid and David began helping me identify potential investments and clients.

Believe it or not, I chose to stay away from involvement in the apparel industry. I had two good reasons. First, I was still very much attached to Liz Claiborne and would have found it hard to help a potential competitor. Second, I think I know too much about the apparel industry and how difficult it is to succeed in it. I found myself impatient with fashion newcomers, and I would often say to those who were looking for seed money, "You're better off asking for money from investors who don't know the fashion industry as well as I do."

But we did invest in some of the new Internet companies, and maybe we should have stuck to fashion. By and large these investments were not successful.

My new life really started when I began to deepen my involvement in philanthropy. My interest in it began in the early day of Liz Claiborne,

1981 to be exact, when my partners and I established the Liz Claiborne Foundation. Our initial goal was to contribute to the many non-profits that traditionally looked to the apparel industry for financial help. Frankly, we could afford to be generous to these organizations.

In the mid 1980s, Simona made me aware of the issue of domestic violence. In her therapy practice, she was seeing many clients who had come to her because of abuse problems caused by their partners. Simona pointed out that abuse, contrary to my original thinking, took place at every socioeconomic level and was a very serious widespread problem for women. I brought my new-found understanding of this issue back to the Foundation board at Liz. We couldn't help but recognize that there must be plenty of abuse victims amongst our own consumers, and we decided that we had to do something to help them. We became involved.

Senator Feinstein at San Francisco domestic violence gathering.

The company itself took a very strong stand on domestic violence starting in the late 1980s, before there was much public awareness of the problem. Not only did we make financial contributions, but we were among the first large corporations to address it directly. We decided that we would have to do something to raise public awareness and to let abuse victims understand that there were places they could go to for help. The young women in our company were all very eager to work on programs to this end.

We decided that since we had such strong relationships with department stores that we should approach them to work with us in their cities and get behind these efforts for the sake of their consumers. We put together an outstanding program in San Francisco and contributed funds for the first domestic hotline in that city.

I like to feel we played some small part in the first Violence Against Women Act which was passed during the Clinton administration. I was asked to serve on the National Domestic Violence Council with social workers, lawyers, judges, police officials, and corporation executives participating. I was happy to devote time to this organization and participated along with people like Janet Reno, the Attorney General, and Donna Shalala, the Secretary of Health and Human Services.

The good news is that The Liz Claiborne Foundation still dedicates virtually all of its funding to organizations that deal with the sources and ramifications of domestic violence. The bad news is that domestic violence still exists.

As I was leaving Liz Claiborne, in fact it was on my last day, I told Paul Charron that I had no intention of lurking around the company, but one thing that was closest to my heart that I didn't want to leave behind was the Liz Claiborne Foundation. The Foundation had grown over the years to an endowment of close to $30 million throwing off about $1.5 million to give away every year. We had grown to the extent that we needed and brought in a professional to be in charge of the day-to-day operations. The board, of which I was an original member along with my three partners, held quarterly meetings and staying on the board would mean my showing up at the office from time to time.

I asked Paul if he would mind if I remained on the Foundation board, which now consisted of a group of executives from many parts of the company. He was very gracious and said "Certainly. Stick with it. Stay with it as long as you like."

I'm happy to say that I'm still with it after all of these years.

The Liz Claiborne Foundation gave me a taste of the philanthropic life, and it inspired me to find other ways to "give back" to the community and to fund organizations I believed in. In 1983, while still with Liz, I started The Chazen Foundation.

My accountant, Bernie Pomerantz, pointed out to me the benefits of a foundation. As a founder of Liz Claiborne, I had a fair amount of stock worth more money than I ever thought I would see in my lifetime. If I set up a foundation and donated some of my stock to it, I would receive two very important tax breaks. First of all, because I was donating something of value, I would be entitled to deduct from my tax return the current value of the stock as a charitable deduction. That would lower my personal tax bill. Plus since I wasn't selling the stock and didn't have to pay taxes on the sale,

I'd end up with much, much more money inside my foundation to give away to worthy causes. Doing good and saving a lot of tax dollars – it's a win-win that doesn't normally happen when dealing with taxes and the IRS.

Obviously, once the stock was in the Foundation, it could no longer be put to personal use. It all had to be given away at one time or another to worthy causes. IRS regulations require that private foundations like mine must give away 5% of its money, its *corpus*, every year. So you can't just let the money sit there and look at it. You have to do something with it. And that's the way it should be.

Funding the Foundation with my stock opened up a whole new world of charitable giving. From the very beginning of our marriage, Simona and I always tried to be as charitable as we could, depending upon our economic circumstances. However, this opportunity to make more meaningful contributions to causes we were passionate about seemed almost heaven sent to me. It gave me my start in my career as a philanthropist – a career that really took off and became the centerpiece of my professional life after I left Liz Claiborne.

Mayor Bloomberg – Holly Hotchner – MAD dedication at City Hall.

With a foundation, I started thinking about charitable giving in a very different way. In the past, like everyone else, I'd have to consider my weekly or monthly income versus my expenses whenever I thought about writing a check to a charity. My personal finances were tied up in the mental and emotional calculations about how much I should give and to whom. It was all different now. I felt suddenly that it wasn't my money any more. It was there to be given away, and my job was to figure out the best ways to give it away. I loved the idea of it.

Simona and I already had a list of organizations that we contributed to: schools, our synagogue, community groups, and other worthy organizations. So while we were always writing checks for $50 or $100, all of sudden we could add some zeroes to the numbers. It made giving more enjoyable, made these organizations a lot happier, and hopefully did a lot more good.

So that's the way we handled our early giving while I was still at Liz, until one day I got a call from Meyer Feldberg, the new Dean of the Business School at Columbia University, who wanted to come in to see me. This was in 1991. I had graduated from the Business School in 1950, and I don't believe that in the 41 years that had passed, anyone had contacted me about becoming involved with the school. Feldberg was going to change all that.

He described some of the new things happening at the Business School, and I was tremendously impressed with his passion for the job. One of the things he was trying to do was establish a Board of Overseers for the school, and he thought that I would be a very good candidate. I agreed to join the board and started attending meetings. We had a very prestigious group of graduates serving, many of whom had achieved considerable success, especially in the financial world. I was certainly impressed with these people, particularly the chairman, Ben Rosen, a venture capitalist who was instrumental in funding Compaq Computers and a host of other famous Silicon Valley companies.

In subsequent meeting with Dean Feldberg, he would discuss what he wanted to accomplish for the school, and one of his ideas struck a very responsive chord in me: He talked about the need to strengthen the school's programs and visibility in international business.

When I was at the Business School, in the late 1940s, by and large there was no real emphasis on international commerce as a necessary part of a business education. The United States had all the raw materials, the markets, the means of production, the know-how, the capital, and everything else it took to create and run successful businesses. We knew that there was a world out there, but at the time we had no use for it. Everything was very USA oriented

In my own career at Winkelman's and later at Liz, Europe and the Far East became vitally important to our companies. I learned about international business on my own, through experience, with no formal schooling at all in the intricacies of international markets simply because the classes weren't available when I was at Columbia.

Of course that had changed over the years, and now, in the early 1990s, it had become obvious that no student of business could ignore the global aspects of the subject. Columbia Business School did offer classes in international business, but Dean Feldberg felt there was more to do. What the school needed, he explained, was an institute that could serve as a focal point for their programs on global business and economics. He said the institute he had in mind would act as an umbrella under which he could consolidate all the international programs. He asked me if I would help him establish such an entity and told me that it would conduct research and offer conferences, serving as a kind of showcase for Columbia's work in preparing its students to do business anywhere in the world.

His idea sounded terrific to me, and I agreed to fund it. Columbia decided to call it the Jerome A. Chazen Institute of International Business.

I pledged $10 million to the project. At the time, it was the single largest gift that the Business School had ever received and one of the largest gifts that Columbia University had ever received. It was also the largest gift I had ever given and represented a good chunk of my net worth. But at the same time I knew the gift would have no effect on my family's standard of living.

I knew that this level of giving, as large as it was, was exactly the right thing to do. It didn't make much sense to me to hang my Liz Claiborne stock certificates on the wall as art, or to line my coffin with them after my death. Suddenly I understood that old phrase, "You can't take it with you." So why shouldn't I make good use of the money while I'm alive? That way, I'd still be around to see it make a difference in the world. I had the resources to do it, and my being a leader in giving just might inspire others to follow suit.

I made the gift in 1991 in the form of an endowment. It has grown over the years, and Columbia gives a portion of it to the Business School every year to operate the Institute.

I'm very, very proud of having made this initial gift, and it did inspire other alumni to step up their level of gift giving. If anyone wants to learn more about the work of the Chazen Institute, they can find its website at www4. gsb.columbia.edu/chazen/.

The gift has kept me closer to the school over these past 20 years than I ever had been before. I am still very involved with the Chazen Institute and work to strengthen its contribution to education in the very global business environment of the 21st century.

Shortly after the announcement of my gift, I received a visit from George Rupp, the president of the University, asking me to consider becoming a Columbia University Trustee. Obviously, my gift had a lot to do with that visit, but in my discussions with Dr. Rupp I learned that the Business School had no trustee representation on the Columbia Board. That intrigued me and made the idea of becoming a trustee very appealing. I joined the board and became very aware of the difficulties of running a university the size of Columbia. I tried to make the best contribution I could during my years of service.

My involvement with Columbia University has been satisfying and fulfilling. As a donor, I've come to realize that as my relationship with the University deepened, my caring increased, and I wanted to do more. I think this is a good lesson for anyone who has any kind of inclination to work with nonprofit organizations: get involved, and as you come to understand the needs of the group, you will want to help in more ways, whether it's giving your time, your money, or your know-how. If you believe in an organization – get involved!

My gift to Columbia did exactly that for me, and more. It altered my mindset completely about giving. Now I wanted to do more – as much as I possibly could. I wanted to figure out how much of my total net worth I could afford to donate to the Chazen Foundation and in turn give to worthy causes. I had become a philanthropist in the real meaning of the word.

Another organization that I began to work with, and which I became deeply involved in over the years is the Museum of Arts and Design in Manhattan. I am the Chairman emeritus of the Museum, which used to be called the American Craft Museum. In the late 1970s and early 1980s, Simona and I started to collect what is called contemporary studio glass –hand blown glass pieces made by a variety of glass artists around the U.S. It was a relatively new collectible that really didn't get it's start until the mid 1960s when Harvey Littleton, who was a ceramics instructor at the University of Wisconsin, and Dominick Labino, an engineer at Libbey Owens Ford in Toledo, Ohio, invented a small furnace that enabled artists to work with and blow glass in their own workshops. With this innovation, the "studio glass movement" was born.

With Jimmy Carter at the University of Wisconsin.

Littleton developed a glass blowing program at the University of Wisconsin and started a course with eight students. These eight went on to become icons of the movement, and each of them moved to other schools, setting up glass art departments. The most famous of these people was a man by the name of Dale Chihuly who in the 50 years since glass has been made this way in the United States has become the symbol of the entire movement. Many people call him the Tiffany of the 20th century.

We fell in love with this glass and started collecting it.

Through our interest in collecting this glass, Simona and I became involved with the American Craft Museum. At the time it was located in a small townhouse on West 53rd Street and was part of an organization called

Jerome A. Chazen

the American Craft Council, an association of craft artists. Within the organization was a little group called the Collector's Circle, and that's what we joined. We would go on trips with the group to visit galleries, studios, and other collectors. It was a fun and exciting few years for all of us as we built collections and discovered new artists.

To make a long story short, in the mid-1980s, the museum traded its home on 53rd Street for a new space on the ground floor of a new office tower. The decision was made to establish a new craft museum in this space. As all of this developed, the American Craft Council realize it did not have the people or resources to support the museum and the decision was made to split into two groups, one to develop and operate the new museum, and the other to continue the work of the Council in furthering the interests of their artist members.. Even though my involvement was relatively new, somehow I ended up as chairman of the museum.

My association with the Museum has lasted now for a rewarding but not always easy twenty-five years. In the beginning, I was faced with a very worthy cultural organization that desperately needed financial help as well as professional management. We needed a director, and we needed people who could do the work of actually putting together the museum in its new space.

I helped get the ball rolling, remained on the board, and became an ongoing contributor to the museum.

In the late 1990s, we realized that the museum, now under the directorship of Holly Hotchner, had run out of space. We also concluded that "American Craft Museum" no longer properly described the new world of "Craft." After a lot of research and discussion, we came up with a new name for the museum to better reflect its mission and the transformation of the Craft movement in this country. We changed the name to the Museum of Arts and Design. Our artists felt that the word "craftsman" did not truly represent their work, and we hoped that the new name would be more fitting for these people. Plus our interest had gone way beyond the U.S., and our collection was now global, so the "American" in the name made no sense anymore and we dropped the word.

We did get some heat from some people in the US craft community, complaining that we were moving away from our traditional mission. But we never intended to move away from it nor have we. Instead, we expanded it, and the change seems to be working very well.

Along with the need for a name change, it became obvious to us that we were out of space to exhibit our growing collection. We were blocked from any kind of expansion because of the physical nature of the condominium space that we were in. We spent some time looking for other locations and fortunately found a small Columbus Circle building where the museum is now situated. We decided that the location would be perfect for us, and it would give us three times the space we now had.

It required a complete renovation – the entire interior had to be gutted and the façade had to be altered. The building of this new museum could probably be the subject of another book. Some people believed that the building had historic value and should not be altered, and they did everything they could to block us by trying to have the building landmarked. We went through an agonizing few years fighting their objections and trying to get the building ready.

I believed wholeheartedly in what we were doing and became Chair of the Capital Campaign, charged with the task of raising the needed funds. As the leader of the campaign, I looked back at what I had done at Columbia University and thought that I should once again make a lead gift that might stimulate other, significant giving. I did it and it worked. Other people began to step up to help, including Nan Laitman, who became in a sense my philanthropic partner in this endeavor, contributing on her own in a big way and also helping to raise money.

Besides being Chair of the Capital Campaign I was also Chair of the Building Committee. We met on a regular basis with the architects to make sure we were getting the kind of building that we agreed we needed. It was a struggle. Plus we had to deal with a full load of other business and legal issues. With all of this plus the fundraising, you could say that taking care of the museum became my new full-time job.

It turned out that cost overruns, delays, and lawsuits made a shambles of our budget, and I ended up more than doubling my contribution in order to ensure that the museum would have this new home. The contribution became my second major gift and a lot more money than I ever thought I would be able to give away. It also made a big dent in the Foundation. But again, I felt that I was doing the right thing and started telling friends that I intended to continue my philanthropic activities and die broke.

Eventually, we raised all the money we needed to get the building built, and we officially opened in October 2008. It's a beautiful space, and the museum has found new life on Columbus Circle. I couldn't be more pleased or more proud to have played a role in making it happen.

The gift – my third major contribution – that really helped deplete the Chazen Foundation is to another museum, this time on the campus of the University of Wisconsin. We have close connections to the University: Simona and I both went there and that's where we met. We were very pleased that our eldest daughter Kathy also decided to go to school there. Louise & Sid's son, my grandson Ross Banon, graduated in 2008, and his younger brother A.J. started at Wisconsin in the Fall of 2010. Kathy and Larry's son, my grandson Zach, will start at UW in September 2011.

Simona had become involved with the University's art museum and became a member of the board. She developed a very cordial relationship with the director Russell Panczenko. It didn't take long for Russell and me to become friends as well. Simona and I see Russell and his wife Paula whenever we are in Madison or on those occasions when they come to New York.

The museum's board met twice a year and sometimes I would go out to Madison with Simona just to visit the campus. We also had some other involvements with the University, including funding a program to bring in a special speaker each year – someone significant who would perhaps offer some master classes or workshops for the students and faculty. The first person chosen was Tony Morrison.

For a while, the program lay dormant, no speakers were brought in, and I was very disappointed. But in 1988 a new chancellor arrived on the scene, a woman named Donna Shalala, and everything changed. Donna later became Secretary of Health and Human Services for all eight years of the Clinton administration. And I became reacquainted with her during those years when we served together on the National Council on Domestic Violence.

Donna came to see me in New York, thanked me for my gift, told me how unhappy she was that the school hadn't been using the funds, and said that she would get the program going again in a big way. She was like a five foot tall fireball, filled with energy and excitement, and we talked a lot about the things she was doing at the school.

Her visit re-invigorated my relationship with the University of Wisconsin. We started spending more time on campus and would go out to Madison to see many of the wonderful speakers they brought in, including Jimmy Carter, Eli Wiesel, Oliver Sacks, and plenty of others. Plus Simona became more deeply involved in the art museum.

A number of years later, John Wiley, who became chancellor in 2001, and whom I had gotten to know and like, asked for a meeting. He talked to me about his concern that the University, while offering a phenomenal arts curriculum, was not well recognized in this area. The problem, he felt, was that the program was spread all over the campus, a building here, and a building there, but no focal point, no real home. His vision was to build an arts campus which would bring all the programs and activities together in one area. The centerpiece of this arts campus would be the University's art museum. The current museum was out of space, and they needed to double its size.

The University Regents liked the plan, he told me, but didn't have money to give to the arts. Their priority was funding science in order to maintain the school's place as a premier science institution. They basically said that he would have to find private money to fund his vision, because they could make no public money available to him.

Chancellor Wiley finished his story, looked up at me and said, "I hope that you might be interested in this new art museum and perhaps give us a lead gift to help get the building built."

I was taken aback. "Wow," I replied, I wasn't expecting anything like this at this meeting." But I told him that I thought his vision was exciting and that if he could really make it happen, it would be a wonderful legacy for my family and myself.

Obviously, both Simona and I discussed this carefully. She was already involved with the current Musem and was passionate about building it to be the best university museum in the country. There were more meetings and, eventually, we got to the issue of money. John gave us a number that they thought would work as a lead gift. It was $20 Million. We gulped and, it became our third major gift.

I then asked John, "When do you think this new museum will be built?"

He replied, "Well, I would anticipate getting the whole job done in 2011 or 2012." He explained that it was a complicated situation because a building had to be taken down, and all the new utilities had to be put in underground, on a fairly crowded campus site.

Well this was 2005, and 2011 was looking like the very distant future. I said, "Well, that might be great for you, but I'm not exactly a kid, and I don't know if I'll even be around for this."

He knew what to say, "Oh no, you'll be around, don't worry about it."

What could I say to that, except, "Thanks a lot!"

Eventually, an idea was floated to allow us recognition now, in case, I guess, we weren't around to cut the ribbon at the opening of the new museum. The plan was to take the old museum, name it "The Chazen Museum of Art" in recognition of our gift, and incorporate the current building into the new building we were funding. We had to get used to the idea of there being something called "The Chazen Museum," but eventually we did, and Simona and I decided to support the project.

The only problem was that the old museum already had a name – the Elvehjem Museum of Art. It had been named after Conrad Elvehjem a famous biochemistry professor who had become the university's president in 1958. He died in 1962.

University officials spoke to the Elvehjem family about the name change and explained that the building would continue to be called the Conrad A. Elvehjem Building, but the museum name would change. Apparently Professor Elvehjem was not really a supporter of the arts, and his family was not concerned. There were a few rumblings in the university community, but really nothing much at all, so the name change went through.

Before construction could start, the whole project almost went off the rails, because the university had trouble raising all the money it needed. At one point the administration had to get back to the Board of Regents with the confirmed budget for the construction along with evidence that they had enough money to pay for it. Well, they didn't have that evidence, they didn't have enough pledges. With the meeting date approaching, I got a frantic call from the Chancellor. We had another talk about money.

"We're going to get the building built, don't worry about it," he said. "But if we can't go to the Board of Regents with the evidence that we have enough money already pledged to it, they won't go along. They won't let us start."

We talked through the situation, and I told him that we had to bring down the budget. Since I was in the throes of the Museum of Arts and Design renovation in New York, I was familiar with ways to try to reduce construction costs. Basically, you can build without finishing every part of the plan, and then you can go back and finish later, when more money is raised. So we decided to leave a few things undone, for example the auditorium, which we would leave as an empty space for now. What usually happens is that once work starts, people get excited about the possibilities – it all becomes more real to them – and they want to get in on it and they contribute.

The point was to bring projected costs in line with the money we did have pledged, so the Regents would green light the project. I sat down again with the chancellor and the director of development, and we looked at the money we had pledged versus what we now needed make the Regents happy. As much as we had cut expenses, it still was not enough. They looked at me, and one of them, I can't remember which, gulped and said, "Would it be possible for you to increase the size of your gift – substantially?" Like, another $5 Million?

That was a tough one, but as they say, in for a penny in for a pound. We spent some time figuring out how we could do this, and then I agreed.

With that additional pledge, along with the cuts we had made, the plan looked good enough to take to the Regents. And sure enough, they gave their permission to get the building started.

Then we had some luck. Because of the terrible state of the economy in 2009, not much building was going on, and the estimates that came back from the contractors were lower than expected. Now we could go ahead and pretty much build without leaving anything out.

The building is now under construction, and they claim to be on schedule, with an opening date of October, 2011. We are monitoring the progress, and the hope is that both Simona and I will be around to participate in the opening.

As I keep telling people, I intend to die broke, but I want to see that museum first.

Besides these very major gifts, Simona and I also work with a number of other organizations. We've been involved with the Lupus Foundation for 30 years, ever since Simona's sister, Naomi Parker, died of the disease. There is also the Metropolitan Opera, where I am a Managing Director. My work there is very fulfilling personally and, very expensive.

Simona and I do have another major music love, Jazz. I discovered Louis Armstrong's music when I first got out to Madison in 1944 and have been a "groupie" ever since. Louis left his home in Queens, NY, to the City of New York, and it has become a museum and an archive. I have been a member of that Institution's board of directors for many years. Simona and I both love the music that Louis played as well as the sounds of many other "mainstream" jazz musicians and, over the years, we have accumulated an extensive library of both jazz books and records. We endowed a jazz series at the 92nd Street Y in New York City to help keep this music alive.

The other side of my philanthropy is community-based. Although I spend a good deal of time in New York City, we have had a home in Upper Nyack, north of the City, for many years. Simona has her office there, where she still practices as a psychotherapist, and I am in Nyack every weekend. Over the years we have become part of the community. We support a number of the local institutions, including VCS, a domestic counseling organization that Simona has been involved in for over 40 years. The Chazen Foundation tries to respond to a variety of needs locally and even internationally, and, as a matter of fact, last year the Foundation contributed to 123 different organizations.

One unintended consequence of my philanthropy is that some community organizations have come to depend on us – perhaps disproportionally in terms of what others could also be contributing. This worries me a lot and sometimes frustrates me. When you give, you don't want to be the only one giving, because then you risk feeling that maybe you're being taken advantage of. It's human nature. You want to help, but you don't want to be the only one doing the helping.

We need to have more people in the community step up and show their generosity – to start sharing a bit of their good fortune with neighbors who are less fortunate. As I've told some of these local organizations, I won't be around forever, and the amount of money in my foundation is miniscule now compared to what it was. In fact, everything that's left in it is already pledged. I've given away a lot, and soon there will be no more to give.

Simona and I are helping our children learn to give back. On the recommendation of my best friend and trusted advisor for many years, Sherwin Kamin, we set up individual foundations for each of them. Now they are developing their own approaches to philanthropy. We have no control over how or to whom they give their funds, but we are very proud of the results.

In these 15 years since leaving my company, I have found that there is as much joy in giving money away as there is in making it – maybe even more. On the other hand, I would not have traded my years at Liz Claiborne for anything in the world. Those years brought me happiness, fulfillment, and the opportunity to take part in this incredible adventure in giving that I am living today. I will always be thankful for that.

Afterword

October 11, 2011

This morning I was putting the finishing touches on the book, when I received the following email.

> Jerry,
>
> We have a mix of good and hard news to announce now, at 8:00 a.m. today. We are announcing that, after a hugely successful launch of the brand last year, J. C. Penney is buying Liz Claiborne brand (and family of brands). Lock, stock, and barrel. They love the brand and recognize that it is the singular game changer to elevate and win the share battle vs. Macy's. Our success can be measured in so many metrics—the best being the number of new shoppers to JCP in the past year that have entered the store looking for Liz.
>
> With the sale of Liz, we are (understandably) required to rename the corporation—something I have been loath to undertake, given the symbolic and meaningful heritage of that name. But the time has arrived, and we will do so in the next 6 to 12 months.
>
> I know you are writing your book now, and this may somehow factor into it.
>
> My best,
> Bill McComb, CEO Liz Claiborne

Wow! I now can really come to closure on my life with Liz. I'm putting these thoughts down as they spin through my mind mixed with 35 years of memories.

I'm not surprised that this happened. The shock came when the original deal was made with J.C. Penney. I knew then that it was only a matter of time that they would exercise their option. I know that it has been a big win for Penney's and I can only hope that they continue the relevance of the brand.

Liz, herself, is gone. Leonard Boxer also passed away. Art survives in his own world and I still relish the thrill of having built a great company.

Thank You

Writing this book has been a very personal and challenging task. The events and the people who were part of those years are so large and varied that it would not be possible to mention them all. A very few are specifically mentioned in the book, but many others, just as significant, are not in these pages.

The truth is that all had a part in my success and the success of the Company.

Running a large, successful corporation means dealing with a variety of functions that somehow have to come together to create the total entity. In the case of an apparel company like Liz Claiborne, Inc., the beginning of everything is the design staff and the creativity that sparks the consumer. Along with the designer, the merchandising people take these ideas and translate them into quantities, groups and products. Production then takes over and, in our case, production was a logistical nightmare. We virtually pioneered the use of overseas facilities and dealt with the vagaries of quota, training of people and shipping our thousands of units from different countries at different times. And of course, the sales people, the servicing people, and the wonderful folks in the warehouse got the job done.

Obviously, as a start-up, there were only a handful of employees. I still remember our first Christmas party at the warehouse where two large pizzas took care of all our food needs. Almost overnight we added hundreds of employees and, in some miraculous way, found dedicated, work 'til you drop, loyal associates. I could never thank these folks enough for what they did. Some are still with the Company, some nicely retired, and some enjoying other jobs in other places. Without them there would be no Company and, certainly, no book.

Behind all of this structure, was our extremely talented finance division. We started the Company with $250,000 in cash; built it rapidly into a multibillion dollar business and never borrowed a penny. The mantra was that overhead chases sales; never the other way around.

The retailers were friends and partners. As I describe in the book, Liz was never just another line for them. Relationships developed in almost every case, going to the very top. There was a shared confidence and mutuality of purpose. Every one of those retail people helped us in so many ways. They were, after all, closest to the consumer, and we tried to take advantage of their knowledge to do the best possible job.

Our manufacturing relationships were also critical to our growth and success. Everything we shipped was contracted and manufactured by suppliers we did not own. As our growth exploded, many of these suppliers invested in equipment and facilities to meet our needs. With our help, they took advantage of new technologies that made the manufacturing process a little easier and more efficient. They too were friends and truly partners.

I just would like to say "Thank you" to these hundreds and, eventually, thousands of people who together were responsible for a phenomenon never before seen or even contemplated.

Index

Dylan, Bob, 19

E

Eaton's, 158
Eccobay, xv, 18–20, 23–24, 33
Echo Scarves, 116
Eddie Bauer, 89
Elisabeth, larger size women's
  division, 130–131
Ellen Tracy, 126, 127
Elvehjem, Conrad, 184
Elvehjem Museum of Art, 184
employees
  domestic, 64
  growth of, 136
  interaction between ones in
    States and ones in Europe,
    163–164
  "Lizify"-ing of, 94
  number of, xviii, 59, 83
  overseas, 59–60
England, 12. *See also* United
  Kingdom
Estee Lauder, 99, 122, 124
Europe, 14, 157, 159, 161, 162–
  164, 177
Evan Picone, 49, 86, 137
experience, importance of, 1
eyewear, 117

F

F. W. Woolworth Company, 167
fabrics
  for casual sportswear pant, 96
  designer-equivalent fabrics, 25
  extras to outlet stores, 71
  Liz Claiborne Collection
    staples, 32

purchased one location,
  assembled another, 83
use of domestic fabrics, 57
use of overseas fabrics, 58
velour, 42–43, **44**, 45–46
Falk, Harvey, ix, 166
Far East, 14, 137, 177
Farah, Roger, 167
Fargo ND, 39–40
Farrell, David, viii, 99, 120–121
fashion industry. *See also* apparel
  industry
  Alan Glen as responsible for
    getting author into, 69
  author's first job in, 19
  founders as having spent lives
    in, xvii
  hard and fast marketing rules
    of, 54
  as important and exciting
    place to be, 105
  new company failure rate,
    xviii
  size of manufacturers in, 51
  as worthy of investment, 101
Fashion Institute of Technology, 31
fashion magazines, 80–81. *See also*
  specific magazines
Federated Department Stores, 8,
  77, 154–155, 156
Feinstein, Diane, **173**
Feldberg, Meyer, **172**, 176, 177
feminism, 26
finances
  initial investment, xviii, 23, 24
  sales figures. *See* sales figures
findings for garments, source of, 59
Finkelstein, Ed, 153, 154, 156
First Issue, 152

R

Ralph Lauren, 36, 37, 97, 120, 122, 148, 167
Randel, Jane, ix–x
Reagan, Nancy, **118**, 119
regional malls, 88, 89
Reiner, Art, viii, 154
Reno, Janet, 173
reorders, compared to brand new merchandise, 48
resort areas, 69
retail executive hiring, as game of musical chairs, 8
retailer(s)
    as customer for manufacturers, 32
    partnership with manufacturer, 80
    training consumers to shop the sale, 145
retailing
    author as natural for, 9
    author's fascination with, 5, 6
    current picture of, 99
    death of traditional approach to full-price retailing, 153
    destruction of, 147
    in Europe, 163
    new business model of, 89
    principles, 31
Rhea Manufacturing Company, 2–6, 20
RJR Nabisco, 153
"road shows" (dog and pony shows), 102
Roberts, Ed, 33
Robinson's Department Stores, 139
Rockaway NJ, 20

Rosen, Ben, 176
Rosen, Carl, 101
Ross, Ken, 137
Ross Stores, 68, 71
royalty income, 114
Rupp, George, **172**, 178
Ruskin, Ron, vii, **76**
Russ Togs Inc., 134
Russia, 14–15

S

Sacks, Oliver, 183
Saks Fifth Avenue (Saks), 13, 33, 41, 43, 45, 77–79, 95, 126, 130, 134, 158, 167
sale crazy, stores as, 99
sale signs, 143
Salem OR, 41
sales
    author as sales manager, 5
    author as salesman, 4–5
    contests, 98
    cut-backs in store sales personnel, 90
    of denim apparel, 119
    goals for, 98
    new approaches needed, 31
    in petites division, 95
    of tops compared to bottoms, 42, 82
    tracking of, 9–10
sales figures
    in Canada, 159
    Dana Buchman line, 127
    Elisabeth, large size women's division, 131
    fragrances, 125
    history of, xviii, 34, 46, 136
    international sales, 164

JEROME A. CHAZEN is one of the four founders of Liz Claiborne, Inc. During his tenure he was largely responsible for the innovative sales, marketing, distribution, and licensing programs that are an integral part of the Liz Claiborne success story. Mr. Chazen is also the founder of the Jerome A. Chazen Institute of International Business, the focal point of all international programs at Columbia Business School. Mr. Chazen is involved in many other business and philanthropic organizations, including the Museum of Arts and Design in New York, and the Chazen Museum of Art at the University of Wisconsin. He also serves on a number of corporate and charitable boards. Mr. Chazen and his wife, Simona, are serious art collectors.

Mr. Chazen received his Bachelor Degree from the University of Wisconsin and his MBA from Columbia Business School. He has lectured at Columbia University, University of Wisconsin, Fashion Institute of Technology, and elsewhere. He has been profiled in Fortune, Forbes, BusinessWeek, Time, Crain's New York, Woman's Wear Daily, Art News, and Lifestyles, among countless others.

In this business memoir, Jerome A. Chazen, tells an extraordinary success story – how, together with designer Liz Claiborne, he took a small startup business and grew it into the largest apparel company in the world.

Chazen is one of the most celebrated fashion executives of all time. Through his inventive management of Liz Claiborne, Inc., he created a company beloved by generations of women who enthusiastically dressed themselves for both the workplace and leisure time in Liz Claiborne clothing and accessories.

In this book, for the first time, Chazen tells the inside story of the founding of the company, the management tactics and strategies he utilized to propel it into the Fortune 500, the internal struggles and tensions that marked the business's phenomenal growth, an inside look at the processes that made Liz a "rock star" in her time, and revealing insights into what it takes to navigate successfully in one of the most competitive industries in the world.

Mr. Chazen shows readers how design and creativity is never enough to ensure success. Only by joining the creative processes to savvy marketing and sales strategies can any company achieve great success. He illustrates how he did it at Liz and shows by example how other companies can do the same and flourish as well.

CPSIA information can be obtained at www.ICGtesting.com
Printed in the USA
LVOW042331080112

262807LV00001B/6/P

9 781467 036047